TROPICAL HOME

Inspirational Design Ideas

KIM INGLIS

Photography by LUCA INVERNIZZI TETTONI

TUTTLE PUBLISHING
Tokyo • Rutland, Vermont • Singapore

Published by Tuttle Publishing, an imprint of Periplus
Editions (HK) Ltd.

www.tuttlepublishing.com

Photos © Luca Invernizzi Tettoni
Text © 2010 Periplus Editions (HK) Ltd

ISBN 978-0-8048-3980-8

Distributed by:

North America, Latin America and Europe
Tuttle Publishing
364 Innovation Drive
North Clarendon, VT 05759-9436 U.S.A.
Tel: 1 (802) 773-8930; Fax: (802) 773-6993
info@tuttlepublishing.com
www.tuttlepublishing.com

Japan
Tuttle Publishing
Yaekari Building, 3rd Floor
5-4-12 Osaki; Shinagawa-ku; Tokyo 141 0032
Tel: (81) 3 5437-0171; Fax: (81) 3 5437-0755
tuttle-sales@gol.com

Asia Pacific
Berkeley Books Pte Ltd
61 Tai Seng Avenue
#02-12, Singapore 534167
Tel: (65) 6280-1330; Fax: (65) 6280 6290
inquiries@periplus.com.sg
www.periplus.com

Printed in Singapore

13 12 11 10
5 4 3 2 1

TUTTLE PUBLISHING® is a registered trademark of Tuttle
Publishing, a division of Periplus Editions (HK) Ltd

CONTENTS

The living room of the Ocampo family home in Manila showcases how the tropical outdoors can be part of the house even when the home is enclosed. Expansive garden views contrast with studied elegance inside. Vintage Carrara marble coffee tables, displaying artefacts by accessory company Celestina, sit before a Florence Knoll sofa.

DESIGNING A TROPICAL DREAM HOME

Most designers agree that a successful design concept for the home includes four key elements: form, function, style and comfort. In the tropical world, form embraces a fluid transition between interior and exterior spaces; buildings that work well with a hot, humid environment; and architecture that both celebrates its setting, yet is suited to the modern world. This is where the function comes in: It needs to work — both as a home and a technical entity.

In the case of function, we don't want fabrics that rot easily in the humidity or lose their color under the sun's harsh glare. Flimsy, wooden furniture that disintegrates under the demands of termites or other insects is a definite "no no"; we're not looking for stuffy spaces with little natural ventilation. Rather, our homes need to be light, airy and bright with adequate cross breezes, beautiful views, and furniture and furnishings that are built to last.

And, if they are comfortable and stylish, so much the better. As it is the tropics we're talking about, we want them to have an equatorial edge, a sense of place, a type of décor that delights in all that Asia has to offer — but isn't harking back to an earlier era. Naturally, we explain how all this translates into the temperate world too — many of our ideas work just as well in a metropolitan European or American apartment as they do in a villa in Bali or Thailand.

Tropical Craftsmanship, Modern Décor

Luckily, the tropical world is perfectly placed to cater to homeowners looking for Asian artifacts because it has a rich history of craftsmanship. In many areas — northern Thailand, Cebu in the Philippines, the island of Bali — whole

Manila-based design firm Celestina is known for taking local materials and producing modern wares with a Western aesthetic. Its abalone shell table and *kamagong* wood dining chairs are a case in point.

communities have traditionally worked in the field of wood carving, lacquer and ceramic production, painting and such like, usually for the adornment of temples or palaces or both. Today, these traditions continue — but in a radically different manner.

No longer are murals reserved for royalty, carvings restricted to images of the Buddha. Rather, age-old skills and techniques are utilized to produce a whole new set of products: homewares, furniture, tableware, furnishing fabrics — sensual and serviceable goods that bring beauty, zest and practicality to the home. Ancient handloom weaving translates into upholstery fabrics with modern geometric patterns in primary colors; lacquer techniques utilizing gold, silver and neons produce zany trays and plates; neo-weaves have been formulated to elevate the ancient chaise into a weather-resistant, super-comfy pool lounger.

The list is endless, the end results enduring. Furthermore, inroads with new forms and materials are allowing artisans to continue doing what they've always done, but with an injection of modernity that sits well with the contemporary home. You may see an Asian motif, a particular pattern, a cultural reference, but it will be incorporated into a super-sexy new dinner service or a richly textured bedspread. Look to pages 92 and 66 for examples of modern-day ceramics and fabrics that honor time-treasured techniques.

In another vein, but on the same subject as it were, there is a plethora of old *objets d'art*, furniture pieces, ancient wood partitions, fabric remnants and more all finding new life in different forms. Embracing sustainability, they're turned into decorative features or are used as parts of cushions, runners and curtains. Antique chests, formerly used to house Buddhist manuscripts, are salvaged, restored and find new use as cabinets to house television and DVD players; old house gables become bedheads; carvings of *nagas* (serpents) from a balustrade or an elaborate monastery roof finial or eave bracket become decorative accents in the home; old carved Balinese doors become centerpieces in a living room. Turn to pages 28, 56 and 62 for some intriguing ideas in this sphere.

Of course, there's nothing new in this recycling of salvaged objects, but it's interesting to note how such vernacular items can sit side by side extremely contemporary neighbors. Karina Zabihi, a Singapore-based interior designer at kzdesigns, advocates breaking the rules, subverting traditions and mixing and matching quite brazenly. She says: "As we move more readily between overseas homes and since the Internet has created a truly global village, our homes have become repositories for our travel-gathering mementos. Seeing a Korean chest in Chelsea or a baroque chandelier in Bali is no longer a rarity, in fact it is all the rage." She sees such contrast as key to a striking interior, as it adds layers of visual interest to a room. A low-slung Italian sofa set, for example, doesn't have to be accompanied by an abstract art piece; sometimes, the sinuous form of an Asian antique carved panel provides just the right element.

As we become more environmentally aware, the key issue is to recycle and re-use. This is increasingly becoming the case in the construction of homes as well as in the décor. A particular proponent of recycling is Singapore-based designer Ed Poole; many of his commercial spaces and homes sport re-used railway sleepers and telegraph poles, for example.

How to Achieve a Stylish Decorative Scheme

We don't simply give lists of stockists and examples of homewares in this book. Rather, there are plenty of tips and ideas about a variety of decorative styles. Dividing the book into six chapters — the living room, the dining room, the bedroom, the bathroom, the tropical pool and the tropical garden — we showcase successful decorative schemes in all six. We discuss color, texture, combinations of objects,

Orienting the glass walls of this Bangkok bathroom to the east ensures that the room is drenched in natural light every morning. A pair of Tibetan rugs adds an injection of color into the white marble interior.

materials, forms and more, all the while giving you examples of various regional and national styles too.

Because designing a home is such an individual process, we don't dictate. Rather we give examples, offer advice, comment and talk about trends, all the while showcasing homes and villas, as well as some hotels and resorts, from countries as diverse as China and the Philippines in the north, to Indonesia in the south, and India, Sri Lanka and the Maldives in the west. The tropics cover a vast area as well as a vast diversity of geography: there are homes in the hills, misty mountain environments, as well as dusty plains and hot, humid sea-level scenarios. Of course, there are apartments in the city as well as dream homes in the rice fields, so many of the ideas can be adapted and adopted in other areas of the world.

Many designers advocate starting with a blank canvas, a neutral scheme, and building layer upon layer on top of this. In the living room, for example, Zabihi advocates using shades of white, beige and creams to create the perfect minimalist backdrop for showcasing artwork or displaying favorite pieces. "Rich colors are so much more emphatic against a white background," she declares, "and even though this can be a bold, difficult look to pull off — especially in the tropics where the colors are generally so robust and vibrant — the contrast between a neutral space and flamboyant Asian colors works a treat." Turn to pages 44 and 38 for our ideas on hot pinks and the ubiquitous Asian orange, as well as our section Neutral Zone on page 32.

Apart from color, there are many other ways in which to add character and visual interest to spaces. Playing with size, for example: placing a tall thin object next to a long, horizontal one or teaming a group of identical objects next to a different sized one stimulates the senses and pulls the eye. Playing symmetry against asymmetry, using reflective surfaces such as mirrors and water (see pages 102 and 130) are two others. Layering with textures — teaming soft materials with hard ones, organics with man-made — adds tactility on a more subtle level. And don't forget the lighting: study how natural light enters a room at different times of the day, and plan the artificial lighting carefully.

Many of these ideas are technical, and even if it is difficult to imagine getting carried away by geometry and positioning of objects, we shouldn't get too bogged down in following formula. Our advice? Get the basics right, then experiment. The home should be more than "a machine for living in", something that Le Corbusier in his business-like way once declared. It should reflect the owner's personality.

The Importance of the Outdoors

Because we are mainly considering the tropics in this book, two chapters are dedicated to the outdoors. We look at loggias and *lanais*, verandahs and decks and the way that semi indoor/outdoor living is inherent in tropical architecture. Courtyards are an integral element in many tropical homes, as are verandahs, pavilions, *salas* and such like. Even in the earlier chapters where we discuss the living and dining room, the bedroom and bathroom, there may be reference to gardens or garden courts. Tropical bathrooms, for example, often have an outside element; our Outdoor Bathing section on page 96 gives ideas both for garden bathrooms as well as enclosed bathrooms that are simulated to look like they're outdoors.

We don't touch too heavily on landscaping — if we were to consider gardens we would be writing another book! — but we do look at landscape elements like pool forms, water features, poolside decking, paving, outdoor furniture and lighting, and more. Top architects and landscape designers, some of whom are considered leaders in their fields, have designed many of the villas featured. In our opinion, old can be the new new (think how hip 1930s Shanghai or retro 1950s furniture is), so we aren't afraid to showcase older homes that have withstood the test of time. Others are fairly recent additions to the tropical dream-seeker repertoire — but all are unified by a commitment to a design excellence that embraces individuality.

In the indoor/outdoor sphere, we turn to Asia's foremost architect Geoffrey Bawa for advice. Bawa's pavilion style has been copied, distilled, distorted and diluted over the decades — but it wouldn't be stretching the truth to say that his influence still lives on. Plenty of his devices can be seen in this book — many of the works by more contemporary architects and designers bear his hallmark blurring of boundaries between in and out — and we even have some photos of his former Colombo office now renovated into a lively gallery cum restaurant (see page 42). And even though Bawa insisted that you couldn't see or explain what he was trying to do with courts, verandahs, pavilions, colonnades and gardens without actually walking through the spaces themselves, we think many of the photos tell a different story.

Another great lover of the outdoors is designer and writer Madé Wijaya, Asia's foremost landscape designer and arbiter of taste in the tropical world. Wijaya advises that landscape and architecture, as well as interior design, should all be formulated together in the planning stages of a project. "All too often," he laments, "the garden is left to the end when the budget has shrunk to nothing." As with Bawa, he advocates treating the outdoor elements with the same care and consideration as are bestowed on the interior.

Says Wijaya: "Even though many recently designed tropical homes and gardens have moved away from the romantic and more towards the formulaic, one can be modern and still poetic. If envisaged carefully, using the artful, natural and ornamental oriental style of Balinese landscapes, one can plan a garden that works beautifully with an indoor/outdoor tropical home." See our chapter on gardens on page 128.

Take Wijaya's landscaping at the Four Seasons in Jimbaran, a resort that comprises a series of interlocking villas, paths, public spaces, pools and water bodies, all fronting a gorgeous Balinese bay. Here, inspiration came from the backyard plantings in the neighboring village of Pacatu — tight clumps of frangipani, pandanus and cactus — which were interspersed with cooling water elements, Balinese village walls, interconnecting pathways and lots of poetic corners. It's an example of how architecture can be furthered by a carefully planned garden. Each individual villa with its own plunge pool offers glimpses of layers of landscaping in front and to the sides, all the while framing views of the bigger picture.

Our living room and garden chapters look closely at such views, picture windows, peepholes and the interconnection of outdoor courts with indoor elements, giving various options as to how the outside may be coaxed into the house (see page 22). It also takes a close look at decoration — local wood (see page 28) and the revolutionary inroads in garden furniture design (pages 136 and 140). The overall message is that inside and outside need to work together, so that different moods may be achieved at different times of the day but — whatever the season or time — all work together in a harmonious manner.

This is because, ultimately, harmony is what we are seeking in the tropical home — or in any home for that matter. Mark Twain once famously remarked: "One may make their house a palace of sham, or they can make it a home, a refuge." We're showcasing refuges and homes in this book: We don't expect you to like all of them, but we do want you to gain inspiration and ideas from at least some of them. If you take some of our suggestions — and use them in your own home — we've done our job.

THE TROPICAL LIVING ROOM

The living room, the heart of the house, deserves more than its fair share of care and attention. Lavish time, expense and luxe materials on it; love it, and you'll be rewarded with a room you love.

In the tropics, ventilation is the key. Although a few of the living rooms we showcase utilise airconditioning and are enclosed, we tend to favor spaces that blur the boundary between inside and out (see left). There's something sublimely sensuous, not to mention appropriate, about engaging with the great outdoors when sitting indoors. This seems doubly important today when we face many issues of sustainability and good practice.

However, we don't want to get bogged down in discourse: we want to embrace individuality, regionality and tropicality. So, we flit from the highly distinctive Vietnamese (colonial/Chinese with a twist?) to high Thai style and oriental opulent. Naturally, we're almost fetishistic about "less is more", so modern and minimalist is never neglected — but let's be clear, white isn't always right. Character and color can be etched on a neutral palette. Similarly, we're not about stylistic rigidity; we want modulated spaces that flow from one room to the next, or indeed from inside to outside.

Open-plan living rooms that make the most of sweeping views are nearly always successful — as long as the interior decor doesn't overshadow the drama unfolding outside. So, how to obtain that relaxed, thrown-together look that in actuality is the result of hard work, planning and an obsessive eye for detail? We try to help with a plethora of tips for color schemes, accents, furniture, fabrics, and more. In addition, many of our ideas are sustainable and responsible; in our book, ethics are becoming the new elegance.

Filipino landscape designer, Ponce Veridiano, is a great proponent of what has come to be termed "tropical regionalism" in his architecture, interior and garden design. In this Laguna living room (his first foray into architecture) he relies on local materials — *sasag* or crushed bamboo for the ceiling, *tinalak*, a type of fabric made from banana fibers, for the overstuffed sofa, locally made bird cages for lampshades, and one solid plank of *dao* wood for the low-level coffee table. The result is a relaxed, homey feel. Moreover, it's harmonious with the giant tree fern scenario on one side (seen) and sweeping garden views on the other (unseen).

MODULAR SOFA
SOLUTIONS

Top Italian furniture brands — B&B Italia, Minotti, Cappellini, to name three of the most popular in Asia — monopolize the local market when it comes to living room furniture. Particularly noteworthy is the modular or sectional sofa, where many individual items may be matched together to form different shapes.

The louche antithesis of the straight-backed English Chesterfield, for example, these European models ooze style and elegance. Eschewing formality (or the stiff upper lip), they tend towards the low-slung. They're relaxed and informal, high on quality with a strict no compromise policy. Upholstered in sexy luxe fabrics or soft leather, they would never consider — for a moment — horsehair!

They also work extremely well with their local counterparts who are increasingly experimenting with organic indigenous materials: fibers made from banana leaves, water hyacinth lianas, rattan, bamboo and the like. Check out our examples here and overleaf: The Italian sofa (or equivalent) acts as the anchor, as it were, of the design; the deck is then bedecked with local pieces — woven armchairs and poufs, Chinese wedding cabinets, glass coffee tables, Burmese artifacts, Asian blinds or fabrics and the like. These complement the sofa's sleek lines by adding color, texture and character.

If you're inclined to recline in this manner, look carefully at the sofa selection. We have some Italian classics, while others are local copies. Either way, they're imbued with an understated elegance, thereby encouraging their more exotic companions to shine.

Right The living room in this duplex penthouse in Bangkok features double-height glass windows that illuminate a u-shaped Italian sofa from Dema facing a Xing Dynasty cabinet from Shanxi. It's a cool East-West combo.

Above A fairly conventional pair of sofas was specifically chosen to highlight the highly individual Hugues Chevalier armchairs in this open-plan living space in an apartment in Singapore. Designed by Calvin Sim of eco-id design consultants, the room is intended as a study in luxe — note the muted, yet rich, color palette, floor-to-ceiling silk drapes, custom-made Tibetan silk rug, singular coffee table design, and antique Buddha head.

Below The apartment of leather designers and manufacturers Vichien Chansevikul and Michael Palmer centers around a large l-shaped living room that adjoins an open-plan dining area and kitchen (unseen). A beautifully polished *teng* wood floor acts as the stage for many of their products: two different styles of pouf, a nest of tables in leather, a two-toned console and a magazine storage box. In front of the tinted windows is a generously proportioned sofa that was crafted to the duo's specifications.

Opposite A "Threesome" rattan and glass coffee table and rattan armchair by Udom Udomsrianan takes pride of place next to a muted sofa.
Left Minimal, yet luxe, this living room designed by kzdesigns in Singapore, features a high ceiling that allows for two horizontal picture windows to bring in views of tropical vegetation. As the palette inside is neutral, the vibrant green palms and shrubs stand out all the more.
Below An über-cool living room in Bangkok mixes a Minotti sofa set with a coffee table made from a Burmese bed and an extensive collection of art hung on sliding screens. On left is *Lotus Pods* by Natee Utarit and, on the far wall, a double portrait of the owner by the same artist.

Above A spacious open-sided living room designed with ethnic artifacts and local materials in Laguna, the Philippines is bordered by bamboo groves and a koi pond for cooling.

Near right An ante-chamber, open on three sides, in the Mandarin Oriental Dhara Dhevi in Chiang Mai, Thailand, illustrates how semi covered areas can be used for tranquil tropical living.

Middle right Traditional Thai teak houses usually comprise a series of separate structures all housed on a *chan-ban* platform on stilts. Bedrooms tend to be enclosed, but living areas are usually in open-sided pavilions as seen here in a home designed by Ajahn Chulathat Kittibutr, one of Thailand's most famous architects.

Far right The Sanur compound of Frank Morgan in Bali features a comfy "living room" in a *balé* or pavilion. A pair of over-sized bamboo sofas designed by Linda Garland sits comfortably beneath the steeply pitched roof.

BRINGING THE OUTSIDE IN

Many tropical homes — at least the ones not contained within fortress-like, air-conditioned confines — are composed of a series of semi-indoor, half-outdoor spaces that act as the owners' living rooms. These can take many forms — pavilions, ie spaces with no walls but an overhanging roof, walled courtyards (open above but secured around), extensions of the home (verandahs, decks, patios, balconies) — all sharing a common architectural language: They're uniquely suited to the hot, humid conditions of equatorial Asia and they represent a type of organic architecture that springs historically from the tropical bungalow archetype.

Sri Lankan maestro, Geoffrey Bawa, was the master craftsman of such interwoven spaces. As his work developed, so did his obsession with linking spaces to create new and unexpected views and venues; by the end of his career, it was almost impossible to distinguish between "inside" and "outside". What wasn't impossible was the composition and journey through the various spaces — how they connected, what they revealed and what was hidden.

The few examples we show here and overleaf illustrate how intelligent tropical architecture links the inside of a home both with its surrounds and within its own confines. Views over oceans, lakes or rice fields and gardens are rarely enclosed; there may be some sliding doors or a low overhang, but often the space is left open so that the landscape can truly become part of the interior. This allows for cross-ventilation, is bioclimatic and supremely sustainable. It also encourages natural beauty to invade a space.

For, at the end of the day, tropical Asia is both supremely beautiful and supremely hot. What better than to build with both in mind? Bawa, himself, often brought not only the garden and the view, but pools, boulders, trees and vegetation into the composition — take a look at the design of the house built by artist, Robert Powell, in Koh Samui (overleaf, bottom left), to see how this idea can be taken to an extreme.

Right An elaborately carved open-sided pavilion (or *zayap* as it is known in Myanmar) is the garden entertainment center in Patrick Robert's Yangon home. Such structures traditionally served as resting places for pilgrims, but function equally well in the tropics as living room equivalents.

Below Architect and artist Robert Powell designed and built his three-room home on the island of Koh Samui around the existing topography characterised as it is by massive granite boulders, ancient ficus trees and steep slopes. The entrance to the "living room" is flanked by two boulders that also act as walls, while smaller rocks act as backrests for day beds on a raised lounging platform.

Above One of several relaxation areas on the vast *chan-ban* verandah of Karl Morsbach's Thai-style home in Bangkok. Made from salvaged teak homes from Ayutthaya, the style is a mix of Thai and Western. Western influences may be seen in the glassed skylights and glass-paned eaves that give access to light but also protect from rain, while low-level triangular cushion furnishing is distinctly Thai. **Right** The home of Catherine Denoual and Doan Dai Tu in Ho Chi Minh City is a study in open, inter-connected spaces. Their brief to architect Luc Vernet was to design a home that kept air conditioning to a minimum. Consequently, the home comprises many open-sided areas, including this outdoor sitting pavilion adjacent the master bedroom. Serviced by breezes, cooled from contact with the pool, and a cement floor based on an old French tile design, the space is open on three sides.

THE TROPICAL LIVING ROOM

Above Kevin Tan of aKTa-rchitects in Singapore was asked by his clients to build a "tropical modern" home attuned to nature. This is exemplified in the living room where a steeply pitched teak ceiling and *balau* wood pillars work with local limestone floors and a roughly-hewn wall and pool adjacent. Contemporary furniture from B&B Italia is mixed with local art and artifacts — as well as the tropical scenario outdoors.

Left Architect Cheong Yew Kuan achieves a distinctly modern look in this family home in Bali, albeit one tempered by an Asian aesthetic. The resin flooring, concrete wall and low-level furniture with soft cotton covers are cool and clean, and the tropical garden is invited in on all sides.

Left A distinctly Lanna-style look is achieved here in this northern Thai pavilion with attractive antique pieces and locally woven verandah furniture.
Below left An expansive lakeside retreat on the outskirts of Bangkok is unashamedly Thai style in conception and form. The ample living room sports sliding French doors that can be opened up to invite views and breezes, or closed for a more intimate teak theme. The furniture is all made from water hyacinth, a durable tropical organic.
Below right A daybed in the home of Ajahn Chulathat Kittibutr, an architect from Chiang Mai who has devoted his working life to preserving northern Thai architectural heritage. Overlooking the Ping River, his home is built from old recycled teak beams. This daybed has been updated with the addition of a cool cotton canopy that takes its inspiration from tented Moghul forms.

THE TROPICAL LIVING ROOM

THE WARMTH OF **WOOD**

The archetypal tropical house is built entirely from wood and other natural materials (ie thatch for the roof); it is easily transportable as it is made from prefabricated wooden units that can be pulled apart and reassembled in another location; it is airy, open, light and built on stilts or piles.

As such, it is the perfect construction for the hot, humid tropics — and is both eco-friendly and sustainable. Unfortunately, not many people build in such a manner any more, mainly because bricks and mortar are more structurally sound and because over-logging has resulted in a dirth of tropical hardwoods. However, many people scour the tropical world in search of such old homes: whether they reassemble them exactly as they were originally built or they incorporate certain adaptations depends on the individuals concerned.

When you come across such a home, the most enduring feature is the beauty of the wood. Golden teak is favored by the Thais as it is resistant to insects and hot or wet weather; *merbau*, *bengkerai* and red *meranti* are popular hardwoods in Malaysia and Indonesia; while in south India teak, mahogany and coconut are generally used. In all these countries, you'll see wooden panels augmented by latticework grilles, coconut matting, windows with louvers or rounded "breeze through" slats for natural fenestration, and carved or painted panels.

If you don't intend to salvage and reconstruct a vernacular house, you can bring warm, wooden elements into your home in a number of ways: old agricultural implements make for eclectic ornaments, as do certain architectural forms — the Thai *chofa*, eave brackets, elaborately carved doors and partitions, balustrades, floorboards, beams and posts, and the like. Team them with restored furniture in the form of wooden benches, loungers and low chairs, as well as chests and armoires. Some of the old colonial pieces such as the planter's chair (see bottom right) are particularly popular. Because the seats are in wicker, they are very cool; and because they're set at an angle, more tilted than the usual chair, they're perfect for serious reclining.

Above left Interior designer, Cindi Novkov, has converted a rambling wooden home in Chiang Mai into a showroom for her clients. Here, on an upper balcony, she utilises soft cotton drapes and pristine cream upholstery to lighten dark toned posts, floor, furniture and balustrades. The over-sized, beautifully textured ornament is an old agricultural implement. **Above right** Gold and purple floor cushions bring an injection of color on to this typical Thai teak balcony. This type of pillow is known as *maun kwan*, literally "axe pillow", referring to the triangular shape that resembles the blade of an axe.

Far left A gilded manuscript chest and low-level preaching chair, both the preserve of the monastery in the old days, find new life in a contemporary home. **Middle left** A simple bench is surrounded by some beautifully carved panels and windows in an old Javanese home. On left is a fine example of delicate fenestration, while behind are a decorated window and a ventilation panel above that also allows for the influx of air even when the shutters are closed. A Tibetan bell hangs from a beam beneath the ceiling. **Left** Wooden shutters and posts are complemented by a convivial seating nook on an upper floor of a Chiang Mai home. Here a trio of planter's chairs, so beloved by colonials, is arranged around a simple round table.

THE TROPICAL LIVING ROOM

Above Classic European furniture brings a sophisticated elegance into this Thai-style home in Bangkok.

Above right Salvaged items here include a Burmese gong beneath the coffee table, a Burmese temple panel above the window, and an ornate eave bracket on the old post.

Right The warmth of the roughly textured wood of an authentic Javanese *joglo* structure that was dismantled and transported across the seas for reconstruction on the island of Koh Samui, Thailand is echoed in the low-level coffee table made from an old block of recycled teak.

Middle right A Chiang Mai home utilises Chinese, Thai and European elements in its decorative scheme. The walls are covered in bamboo weave mats, while the textiles come from Studio Naenna, a firm that is dedicated to preserving traditional northern Thai weaving techniques.

Far right Wooden walls, windows and ceiling are lightened by the fresh color palette of the upholstery here.

TROPICAL **HOME**

It's good to mix things up a bit too: aged wood works well with terracotta tiled floors, blue-and-white jardinières and Chinese stools, whitewashed walls, rush mats and soft handloom textiles either in indigos or whites. Because wood retains the energy of its original living organism, it has multiple grains, patterns, tones and textures. Play with these when deciding on your overall decorative scheme. Color-wise, it's a good idea to enliven all that dark warmth with something lighter: blue-and white, cream and orange, a soft celadon. Give the wood pride of place, but don't allow it to dominate with a heavy, moody feel.

The previous pages focused on some special furniture pieces: here, on left and below, we depict some wonderful examples of seemingly living, breathing vernacular wooden architecture. With the exception of the home below, all the photos showcase living rooms in Thailand where it has long been the habit of Thais and foreigners alike to restore and rebuilt traditional Ayutthyan houses. As they were originally built to be easily transportable, this isn't as difficult as it sounds. You simply dismantle the home, pack up the teak panels and take them to a different location for reassembly.

Certainly glass, steel, bricks and mortar all have their place in the 21st century home, but, when we crave for something more organic, wood comes into its own. Thankfully, judging by the current interest in and desire for sustainability, this revival of Asia's wooden heritage — be it in clones, copies or reconstruction — seems set to stay.

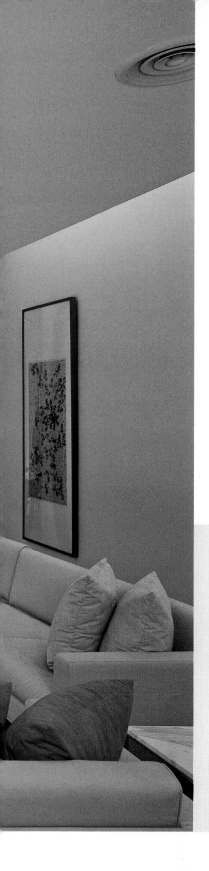

NEUTRAL ZONE

A neutral color palette is a timeless thing; never going out of date, it can retain its freshness with only minimal tweaking. Because it offers a blank canvas, as it were, it is the preferred choice of many a designer.

The trick to neutrals is to vary the textures of fabrics, floor and wall coverings, and furniture. If all the furniture in a room is covered with one texture, cotton for example, it will lack dimension and warmth. So go for a variety of finishes: Suede with cotton, linen with rattan and woven seagrass, wood with glass. For a richer layered effect, add patterns too: stripes, embroidery and appliqué in fabrics; different grains, textures and tones of wood; a feature wall with an unusual finish.

It's easy to find contrasting textures in natural, tropical materials because of the plethora of plant life. Designers regularly use organic weaves in their furniture lines: rattan, cane, wicker, banana fibers, bamboo and hemp often find their way into innovative, individualistic furniture pieces. When teamed with some of the different hardwoods and paired with handwoven fabrics (again in multiple different weaves), the overall effect is super-rich.

Contrast can be furthered by the placement of objects too. Put a tall standing lamp next to a long thin chaise longue or a vertical painting next to a low chair. Mix it up a bit, with pairings of circular and geometric, square and amorphous. This way, your room gains visual depth and interest.

And, if you want a radical room change, it's easily accomplished. Paint one of the walls a striking color, drape a couple of bright throws over the backs of sofas, add some neon-colored scatter cushions, or replace a subdued black-and-white print with an oversized, zany artwork. The overall atmosphere will be changed in an instant.

Left A Singapore home designed by eco-id design consultancy is pristine in shades of cream, taupe and white. The enormous living room is enlivened by a vibrant blue pool and stands of bamboo outside.
Right A seating nook that combines contrasting textures beautifully. The winged Ruben sofa from Padua International is a mix of *abaca* fiber and soft cotton, while the shaggy Natuzzi rug, wooden trellis window and lookalike cane table add further layered dimensions. The coffee table is actually made from a polypropylene resin, so is suitable for outdoor use.

Above The living room in this Kuala Lumpur home is notable for its simplicity and lack of ornamentation. Rather, character is achieved through the architect's use of materials: *balau* wood for pillars, blocks of granite both within and without, and cool limestone floors. Ernesto Bedmar of Singapore-based firm Bedmar & Shi took note of his client's request for a "contemporary but not overpowering home".
Right Wood and white make for calming bedfellows in this villa at Coco Palm Bodu Hithi in the Maldives.
Far right Serenity is the name of the game at Shreyas Retreat near Bangalore in India where the living room is a picture of cool and calm. Silver vessels and ornaments give the room a sense of place.

Above Pale wood, floors and furniture are brought into sharp focus with the addition of a modern black plastic armchair from X•TRA Living. Karina Zabihi of kzdesigns was going for a "futuristic" feel here.

Above Textures play a key role in this seating arrangement: The sofa is made from woven *tinalak*, the cushions sport leafy appliqué patterns in coconut beads, and the giant planters are made from woven rattan.

Above The lofty, vaulted ceiling, imposing columns and the room's airy proportions give this palatial reception room its feeling of grandeur. Add to this, an antique chandelier, a particularly fine collection of Vietnamese shiny lacquered furniture, a family altar, as well as a pair of elaborate Chinese lamps with ceramic elephant stands — and you have all the elements that conjure up the exotic East. The fact that the house is on the outskirts of Hanoi overlooking West Lake helps too! A labor of love, the renovation and rebuilding took owner Loan de Leo Foster a number of years to complete.
Right When working with strong colors, such as gold, red and orange, it's a good idea to focus on the balance and proportion of the ensemble. Here, the perfectly symmetrical arrangment of low-level seating flanked by a pair of lamps with classic vase bases and backed by a trio of gold-leaf panels is strictly geometric.

EASTERN OPULENCE

Asia has a rich tradition of artisans, producing a plethora of goods, ranging from ceramics, basketry and textiles to lacquer, metal and wood wares. In past times, the highest quality of these were reserved for religion and royalty, but, with adjustment in social mobility and economic advancement, many are now available to one and all. Not only is this re-cycling attainable, it is sustainable also.

Even though many such pieces are constructed totally new, you'll find talented teams renovating old wares and selling them on. Chinese wedding cabinets, with reconstituted glossy lacquer and shiny brass bolts, conceal television and DVD players; Buddhist manuscript chests store linen; old thrones and preaching chairs are transformed into elaborate ottomans; and antique textiles double up as screens. Smaller items, such as Buddha images, offering bowls and the like make for atmospheric accents.

Many people prefer to keep such items to a minimum in a modern interior, perhaps placing a Burmese *hsun-ok* atop a Scandinavian-style table or an inlaid glass panel in a boxy display niche. Others have very different ideas, however. They're intent on creating a sumptuous look that should be nothing less than opulent and certainly nothing but Eastern.

In addition to choice artifacts, it's important to get the color scheme correct. Red and gold are the colors of choice, and bright yellows or ochres too (yellow was the color reserved for emperors in China). Surfaces should be highly polished, shiny, glitzy and gilded; northern Thai gold *laai kham* stencil work works well in this type of interior. Go for high ceilings with large sculptural lights, burnished teak gleaming on all surfaces, and suitably exotic, high quality fabrics.

If you're interested in this eastern-emporium style, Chiang Mai is definitely the town to head for. In the past, tightly-knit communities of craftsmen were dedicated to producing beautiful elements for Buddhist temples. Today, with the same commitment and reverence, they carve, weave, weld, work and paint for anyone who is willing to pay for their wares.

Above Mixing and matching nationalities, this reception nook in Vietnam features a Japanese scroll, two Vietnamese lacquered panels depicting the four seasons, 19th century colonial furniture, a Chinese-influenced day bed, Chinese calligraphy and Vietnamese embroidered cushions. The statue of Ba Chua, a prosperity goddess from southern Vietnam, is particularly fine.

Above Shasa Villa in Koh Samui, designed by Palmer & Turner with Leo Design in Bangkok taking care of the interiors, is one of the island's most upscale contemporary residences. This relaxing seating area features outsized furniture designed by Rangsan Narathasajan, a young energetic furniture designer from Bangkok. Custom made to mimic the shape of a large stone that is found on the site, it is enlivened by bright orange and pink cushions. The sculpural heliconia and metal arrangement is by florist to the stars, Sakul Intakul.

Opposite top This home in Bangkok utilises bright, predominantly orange colors, to create a quirky, cheerful interior. Mixing tribal art from Africa with Asian pieces, the collector owner creates interconnected spaces that act as a gallery-cum-home. The contemporary painting by Malaccan artist, Charles Cham, is flanked by a pair of modern Italian armchairs, while the large wooden sculpture on right is by Thai artist Khun Saiyart. Moroccan tribal rugs exude warm, earthy tones.
Right A small seating room in the same home mixes tribal with modern; the muted orange color scheme extends onto the pillars here, thereby uniting this area with other parts of the interior.

TANGERINE DREAM

It could be argued that orange is the color of the East. Some say it is a sign of auspiciousness and spirituality as it represents the ripening of the spring crops. Others declare it originated from the earth, so should be revered — think of ochres, terracottas, rich golden hues, all earthy tones.

Whatever the significance, the color is ubiquitous throughout the region: South East Asian monks' robes are saffron-colored, originally dyed with earth pigments, while in India bright orange marigolds are seen at every turn. Marigold garlands are often given to welcome visitors or adorn a home altar and the blooms are placed on little leaf boats with an oil lamp at evening *aartis* (prayer rituals). Warm coppers and magentas bring to mind tropical sunsets and you'll see deep burnt sienna threads in many a tropical fabric.

Such tones suit an interior scheme in the tropics. Bright sunlight brings out their brilliance, so they work well as accents — scatter cushions, sculptural floral arrangements, a covering of antique embroidery, the backdrop to an ornamental niche. Also, terracotta tiles, along with the red oxide floor "paint" so favored by the colonials, are often used on verandahs; both are cooling underfoot, despite their richly seductive sheens.

Barefoot, a company that has revived rural handweaving practices in Sri Lanka, is synonymous with ochers and oranges. Simple rectilinear forms and bright swathes of color characterize its fabrics; you'll see them in many of the island's upmarket hotels and restaurants. They're now availably globally too: instantly recognizable, they bring a vibrance and sense of happiness to an interior.

VIETNAM EASE

In the past couple of decades Vietnam has opened up considerably, thanks to its policy of *doi moi* (open door). This has resulted in the attraction of foreign investment and outside influences, as well as a type of internal cultural renewal. Old crafts and skills have been revitalized, as the Vietnamese (and expatriate residents) have begun to look to the past to build for the future. The resulting renaissance — in the fields of fashion, art, design, architecture, and arts and crafts — draws on numerous elements in Vietnam's history.

Homes, be they in apartments or old edifices, restaurants, hotels and resorts are springing up, many sporting a sensibility that has come to be called "Indochine style". Collectibles from the colonial era, especially 1930s art deco pieces, sit side by side with more traditional items — the family altar, heavy Chinese-style furniture — and, increasingly, newly-constructed pieces that are modern or "Western" in form but draw on Vietnamese craftsmanship. The resulting mélange is both inherently Vietnamese, yet strikingly contemporary.

Embroidery and lacquer work are very ancient skills in Vietnam, the former dating from the 12th century and the latter going back at least 2,000 years. Today, both are experiencing a revival, as is another old craft, that of celadon ceramics. The same can be said for furniture design: be it a lovingly reconstructed art deco piece or a new model in water hyacinth, rattan, lacquered bamboo or sand-blasted aluminum, it displays an essentially Vietnamese character — one that is easeful, elegant and, ultimately, unique.

Above far left The paneled smoking room in a 1920s villa displays sensitive period restoration with repro ceiling lights a particular delight.
Above middle This living room serves as a repository for contemporary Vietnamese art; the clubby furniture came from France.
Above Both the celadon tiles, made in a factory outside Hanoi, and the furniture custom made by the designer Le Cuong illustrate how Vietnam's tradition of crafts continues to flourish today.
Below left Repro 1930s style leather furniture mixes with Chinese pieces in this clubby Indochine-style room.
Below Family portraits are displayed above a superb French sideboard that was rescued from the French Consulate dining room when it underwent refurbishment.

Right The product of a group of creative cognoscenti, including Geoffrey Bawa who was responsible for the renovation and extension of the buildings, Club Villa is representative of all that is "right" on the Sri Lankan current design scene. Semi indoor-outdoor interiors are sensitively decorated with Barefoot cottons echoing the color of monks' robes, numerous replicas of the 8th–9th century Lankan bronze statue of the *bodhisattva* Samantabhadra, and plenty of period furniture. The overall feeling is of sequestered ease. No wonder the small hotel is seen by many in the know as a place of refuge away from the crowds.

SERENDIPITOUS **SRI LANKA**

Shaped like a teardrop off the south-eastern tip of India, the fascinating island of Sri Lanka has a rich and varied history, matched by a unique style of art, architecture and design. Layered by influences from both Buddhism and Hinduism, and to a lesser extent from its Muslim and Christian inhabitants, the island also retains vestiges of its past Portuguese, Dutch and British colonists. Coupled with a vast diversity of geography, it has a charm all of its own.

Open-air courtyards and innovative stone masonry characterized early Sri Lankan houses — free flows of air were necessary in its hot, humid climate and water was often employed as a cooling element. The Portuguese introduced the covered verandah (see pages 136–139) and high-pitched terracotta roofs, and there are many later classically-inspired Dutch and British bungalows still extant. Developments in the 20th century — especially in relation to Geoffrey Bawa, the country's (and tropical Asia's) most famous architect — also resulted in many homes, hotels and villas of exceptional beauty.

Muslim traders once referred to Sri Lanka as Serendib, from whence the English word serendipity is derived, and certainly the island has more than its fair share of happy surprises as regards its architecture and interiors. A selection is shown here. All share the characteristics we have come to expect of Sri Lankan architecture — copious overhangs, ample verandahs, internal courts with ponds, terracotta tiles, colonnaded walkways, latticed fanlights, and more. Similarly, they are furnished with characteristic heavy Anglo-Ceylonese and Dutch period furniture, as well as some newer woven rattan and cane styles.

Today, Sri Lanka is also famous for its decorative and visual arts scene: somewhat of a secret internationally, it produces some very high quality items on the home furnishings front. If you want to reproduce this type of feeling at home, pair swathes of handloomed fabrics in bright natural dyes and naïf geometric patterns with heavy, dark-stained furniture in tropical hardwoods. Tea chests, planters' chairs, sturdy benches and almirahs in jakwood, ebony or satinwood were built to last; if antiques are unavailable, there are plenty of replicas still being made.

Above and below right Two seating areas in the Sindbad Garden Hotel at Kalutara refurbished in the early 1990s by Geoffrey Bawa and Rico Tarawella, display a strict linearity coupled with contemporary furniture modeled on a boxy colonial design. As is usual, local materials are key here.
Below At Club Villa, a highly polished Dutch chest sits in front of a wall displaying an exuberant mural of tropical vegetation by painter Laki Senanayake.

Above Owned and designed by Udayshanth (Shanth) Fernando, Gallery Café is an exquisite open-air restaurant-bar with adjoining art gallery housed in the former offices of legendary architect Geoffrey Bawa. Many of Bawa's innovations have been retained (his old work bench is now a table in the bar); this seating niche is typical of Fernando's commitment to "looking after every detail" in design.

THE TROPICAL LIVING ROOM

PRETTY IN **PINK**

Pink is symbolic of welcome, love and marriage in Asia, and is considered a color in harmony with the female or *yin* side of life. As such, you'll see it used fairly often in decorative accents in the home — pink cherry blossom scroll paintings, pink silk lanterns, pink and yellow ceramics, for example — but you'll rarely see it used as a total scheme.

Of course there is the famed Pink City of Jaipur in India, but, in reality, its architecture is more terracotta-colored than pink. If it actually was pink, it would be overwhelming. For pink is an extremely strong color and it should be used sparingly, even with caution. Having said that, a feature wall in a deep magenta, fuchsia or redcurrant can be stunning (but these tones are really where red and pink meet). The one you have to be especially careful with is bubble-gum pink. It may conceivably work in a boudoir or a bedroom, but it's not living room material.

Materials, however, can be pink in the living room. Vibrant pink saris, shot through with gold or purple, wafting in the breeze at French doors, translucent cerise silk and velvet scatter cushions, bold pink stripes in upholstery — all can make a dynamic statement, especially if they are offset by pale bleached wood, neutrals in the furniture and eggshell walls. Lamp shades in Chinese silk with dark wood bases bring to mind 1930s Shanghai, while tall vases of deep pink peonies are timeless and very Asian.

As a splash of psychedelic or a sprinkle of spice, pink can be an exuberant accent color. Redolent of the exotic East, it works well with other dazzling colors — jade, lime green, gold and a spectrum of neons, to name a few.

Above left The studied neutrality of the décor in the home of Ou Baholyodhin contrasts with bright pink crowns of lotus arranged by Sakul Intakul in shallow hand-beaten steel bowls.

Above middle White concrete walls and floor, and rug and furniture in neutrals form the perfect backdrop for this statement-making pink lacquered coffee table. Accessories in the form of rose-colored acrylic lamp, vase and scatter cushions complement. All from Gaya Design.

Above right Fashion-forward Park hotels in India favor eye-catching interiors as evidenced by this rose-tinted seating cluster in Delhi.

Right A hand-embroidered cerise throw brings out the pretty in pink color of the girl's dress in the painting behind. Velvet, silk and hand-bleached cotton cushions from Song Design.

Far right The form of Filipino modern chaise, the redcurrant neo-weave Ovo-Celia, echoes the swirls of the painting and the elegant curve of the Arco lamp behind.

SLEEPING IN
THE TROPICS

Asian bedrooms tend to celebrate the multi-layered, richly textured look so popular with today's designers. With its starting point the romantic net-draped four poster bed, this is hardly surprising. Add to this, the plethora of different textiles produced in the region, and you'll find it easy to create a decorative, yet practical, room.

Our advice is not to hold back. Rather, give your creative juices full rein and indulge your fantasies. After all, the bedroom, together with its en suite bathroom, is the most private room in the house. As such, it can become an extension of your innermost desires, a coccoon-like space for all those dreams you've had — and are going to continue to have.

Texture, as usual, is key. Eschew austerity for luxe fabrics — velvets, chiffons, muslin, organzas, silks — and run your hands over them before you buy. You'll want a super soft, sexy and sensuous feel for plump pillows and throws, while drapes and hangings should be gossamer light and floaty. They need to catch the light and cast shadows around the room — try some of the newer technologically advanced creations with metallic threads. As for sheets . . . go for Egyptian cotton with the highest thread count you can find. Compromise just isn't acceptable in this department.

Lighting is another crucial aspect. Because you'll often be inhabiting the bedroom after dark, you want to create moody lighting with dimmers, but also have state-of-the-art bedside reading lamps. Experiment with wall sconces; they'll throw the light up to the ceiling for a softer feeling. Another good idea is an automatic light for the wardrobe.

We showcase a number of different looks in this chapter, giving tips for both hardware and software, as it were. After all, what is more dramatic than sensuous linens, ornate carving, exquisite embellishment and soft, soothing comfort? Turn to the following pages for plenty of suite dream ideas.

An all-wood interior in a bedroom at the Four Seasons Chiang Mai is characterized by northern Thai textiles, furniture and decorative detailing. The use of ethereal, airy fabrics prevents the room from becoming too "heavy"; rather it retains richness, but looks spacious, light and welcoming.

Above The 17th-century Braganza House, one of Goa's grandest colonial mansions is still occupied by two branches of the Braganza family and maintained to a very high standard. Its rooms display the Goan ability to reinterpret both Portuguese and Far Eastern forms — as illustrated by the superior inlaid flooring, peacock fantail detailing above the doors and, of course, the ornate, heavy four poster bed.

Above right A Spanish colonial four poster from the Philippines is decorated with traditional crochet and lacework in soft cotton. The sweet china pitcher and mirrored stand is also an original.

Right An elaborately carved four poster from a villa at the Ayana in Bali is decorated with sumptuous olive-colored silks, a theme taken up in the Roman blinds and lampshades as well.

Middle right An elegant bed with slender posts dating from colonial times in India dominates this bedroom in an old Maharajah's palace. The "roof" is covered in soft velvet and the runner and cushions are from Venetian firm Fortuny.

Far right A Burmese four poster bed that dates from Victorian times has been updated by slightly lightening the wood through sanding and adding white netting for a casual feel.

OLD-WORLD GLAMOR
FABULOUS FOUR POSTERS

Many of the antique four poster beds that can still be sourced all over Asia have their roots in colonial times.
Some of the most impressive date from the mid 1800s when the British Raj was at its height — but earlier Portuguese, Spanish and Dutch originals are also quite beautiful.

Usually constructed in the Victorian style from hardwood, often mahogany or rosewood, many were made to be "flat packed" so they could be easily transported on military exercises or to the hills where families moved in the summer months to escape the heat of the plains. Many sport elaborate headboards, carved with emblems, shields, crowns, coats-of-arms and the like. Originally, these beds would have been covered with a mosquito net, but if you're using them in temperate climes, they look regal and romantic with muslin or velvet drapes.

Classic Indo-Portuguese homes in Goa with expansive *balcãos* (balconies) were often furnished with heavy day beds for afternoon snoozing, while the 17th- and 18th-century *landhuis*, constructed by Dutch East India Company personnel in former Dutch colonies, was often a treasure trove of heavy Dutch period furniture. In Sri Lanka, Western-style four posters in satin, ebony, calamander and old jakwood, so favored by the Burghers, are still very popular.

It is still possible to buy both original and repro four poster beds in these former European colonies and through the Internet. A bedroom, furnished with such an imposing bed, needs to be spacious and airy. All the better, too, if you use period floor tiles, appropriate decorative details (mirrors, sets of brushes and combs, lights) and heavy pieces of matching furniture, such as an old armoire, as well.

Above A somewhat Japanese aesthetic is achieved in this home's guest bedroom with dark stained wood raised platform bed with futon, a bamboo stencil, and delicate Roman blinds with abstract floral pattern. The interior designer was Karina Zabihi of kzdesigns.

Right A discreet bedroom is partially concealed behind a Chinese moon gate screen carved in dark wood in this sumptuous Vietnamese home. Even though the screen is new, the rest of the woodwork (beams, windows, louvers) are all originals. A degree of privacy is attained with the use of gauzy white drapes.

MONOCHROME MAGIC

The much-vaunted duo of black paired with white is not only a timeless design classic, it is extremely contemporary as well.
Recent examples of innovative black-and-white uses include the utterly beguiling infrared photographs of Angkor Wat by Martin Reeves, Diane von Furstenberg's black and white print dress for Spring 2009, and the decorative scheme in Karl Lagerfeld's Paris apartment.

Older proponents abound as well. Elsie de Wolfe, commonly considered America's first professional interior decorator, was a lady who simply adored black and white. In her seminal book *The House in Good Taste* (1915) she declares, "One can imagine nothing fresher than a black and white scheme in a bedroom with a saving neutrality of gray or some dull tone for rugs, and a brilliant bit of color in porcelain." She goes on to suggest combinations of a white-walled room with white woodwork and a black and white tiled floor; a black lacquer bed and chest of drawers and chair; glass curtains of white muslin and inside ones of black and white Hoffman chintz. Of course, as today's designers and home owners are aware, the possibilities are endless.

Certainly, the examples we showcase are handsome in the extreme. White enlarges a room, while black accents add drama. Dark-toned wood on bedsteads, posts and floors are warm and inviting, while iron is another option to consider. Bold black and white prints on bed linens and cushions are also striking: the Finnish company Marimekko uses the contrasting colors in a wide range of bedroom sets. It also pairs the sets with custom-made lampshades in either drum or chimney shape for that extra touch of style.

Play around with the black-and-white concept at home: remember to aim for a restful feel with plenty of space and lightness to facilitate a good night's sleep.

Above A black mesh screen designed by Lawson Johnston and the addition of grey stripes painted on the walls adds texture and interest to this rather small bedroom. The rich bed linens in silk and cotton are from Gaya Design.
Far left Dark stained wood pairs nicely with soft white cotton in this spare, yet luxurious, bedroom. The simple framed bed benefits from the stacked wood sculpture at its head, while slatted wood cupboards continue the woody theme.
Left This deceptively simple bedroom is a calculated study in geometry. From the half black/half white print on the wall, to the three-quarter length striped curtains and the faux fur runner, as well as the round lampshade of course, it evokes an atmosphere of order and calm. The textures make the bed cosy, but the strict linearity of the soft furnishings prevents it from becoming sloppy.

Above Bamboo and cotton, bleached floorboards and voile curtains . . . this bedroom ensemble is light, airy and ever so slightly disheveled. Fold-away bed and fine-woven linen are from Esprite Nomade, a company that specialises in a type of eco-chic camping look.

Right Simplicity as luxury on a private island in the Indian ocean: With a sandy floor and a structure made entirely from coconut thatch, wood and fronds, this is about as basic as you want to get.

ROBINSON CRUSOE NIGHTS

The penchant for experiencing a tropical night in the raw, close to nature and the nighttime elements, is an increasingly popular holiday option amongst stressed-out urbanites. Preferably situated on a private island with endless sandy beaches and swaying coconut palms, the experience can be exhilarating and exciting — sort of back to basics, but with an inherent and necessary level of comfort included.

The accommodation needs to be constructed from natural, not man-made, materials. Wood, thatch, palm fibers, bamboo, adobe and roughly-hewn stone are all suitable; they're rustic enough, but also offer decent shelter keeping tropical rain and sun at bay. Furniture should be country style and give the impression of being "thrown together", but in actuality is robust and practical. Think teak platform beds, diaphanous mosquito netting hanging from the rafters, large clay urns and bamboo spouts for showers, and the like.

The trick here is to give the impression of impermanence, of castaway camping à la Robinson Crusoe. Recreating the look at home can involve opening out windows and doors to allow breezes to enter, decorating with natural organics, using ethnic weave fabrics, flooring in rush or sisal matting and integrating some hand-crafted furniture into the décor. For paint finishes, try some sponging in pastels or a utilitarian whitewash.

The overall look should be simple and uncluttered, but nonetheless warm and inviting with copious use of wood. An added bonus is that creating a secluded hideaway ambience is easy on the pocket — unless you're factoring in a private island cost as well!

Above Beachcomber chic: A simple accommodation at the so-called Spider House on the idyllic island of Boracay in the Philippines. Here, a number of simple huts, all built from found materials, are rented out to sun-searching escapees from the city; the laidback experience is about as attuned to nature as you can get.

Below and right Woven coconut fronds are both sustainable and hardwearing for roofing, doors and "windows". When used in this manner they allow breezes to enter, but keep bugs at bay. The addition of mosquito netting is advised as well; in a Western interior, diaphanous white tulle drapes can be teamed with soft cottons and driftwood accents.

Right A rustic home in Doi Sakat, Thailand features a back-to-basics bedroom with bamboo framed bed, woven walls and minimal furniture. It may be low on amenities, but it has a high eco ethos.

Right and below right Six Senses is a resort and spa company that doesn't wear its environmental credentials lightly. Putting their money where their mouth is, they built this resort on a small island in Nin Van Bay, Vietnam entirely from natural and recyclable materials. The overall effect is similar to life in a Vietnamese village — but with modern plumbing and high quality cuisine.
Below More scenes from Boracay's Spider House.

THAI STYLE, **HIGH STYLE**

Proponents of traditional Thai style will love these bedrooms, ranging as they do from the authentically vernacular to lightly Thai accented. All utilize wood in one form or other, many feature temple forms created by master craftsmen, while others combine antique pieces with contemporary influences.

The results are highly textured, multi-layered and rich with detail. Recycled wood or wood taken from renewable sources is sound, while textiles, more often than not, are sourced from the high-end Jim Thompson atelier. With a slightly rough texture, Thai silk is heavier than Indian or Chinese silk, so is especially suited for soft furnishings. In addition, Jim Thompson patterns are often inspired by traditional Thai motifs.

Recreate high-style Thai opulence at home with some key pieces. The oft-seen triangular wood carving incorporated into a furniture item or hung as a stand-alone wall feature is most likely a temple or house gable; the more intricately carved ones often sport gilding as well. With floral or vegetal motifs, they make for attractive ornamentation. Similarly, screens, pillars, posts and old religious objects, such as manuscript cabinets, offering trays and altar seats, add an element of Thai-style glamor to a room. Be it an architectural remnant or a specially crafted reproduction, as long as it is recycled, it is both aesthetic and ecologically friendly.

Increasingly, Thai style is becoming synonymous with sustainability. With teak, mahogany and other hardwoods in short supply and all wood sources diminishing daily, recycling existing pieces is more than simple common sense. It also provides employment for craftsmen, keeping age-old skills alive. Entire communities, especially in northern Thailand, have been given over to turning temple brackets into table bases or carved panels into cabinets, thereby benefiting the populace both socially and economically.

When combined with floaty drapes, gorgeous silk bedspreads and intelligent lighting, the warmth of Thai wood comes into its own. With its seductive curves and detailed forms, it works extremely well in today's refined bedrooms.

Left above and below The combination of richly carved wood and cream-colored drapes proves beguiling in both these bedrooms. At the head of the top bed we see a gable from a northern Thai temple; on left is a carved eave bracket.

Above The sybaritic surrounds of the Royal Villa accommodation at Mandarin Oriental Dhara Dhevi in Chiang Mai illustrate how a high-end Thai style interior can be achieved. Solid pillars are decorated with gold leaf stencilling (*lai kham*), a craft first perfected in northern Thai temples, while the four poster bed sports gold and burgundy Thai silk covers and cushions. Wood is highly polished, ceilings lofty and the en suite bathroom with cavernous bath suitably sizeable.

Below left An antique Chinese-influenced bed, along with high-end Thai art and furniture, presents a formal look in this bedroom at the Jim Thompson house, Bangkok. Naturally, the silks come from the eponymous atelier.
Below right Opulence is the name of the game here with a low-level platform bed integrated into massive structural posts. The addition of scarlet drapes, gold statuary, silk-shaded lamps and intricate Pakistani rugs raises the design bar.

Left A simple twin room receives a makeover with an injection of color and pattern on one wall. The look designer Joy Dominguez was going for was "vintage glamor", achieved most specifically with the repeated pattern of a group with parasol. **Opposite** One feature wall covered with Thai-style gold stenciling avoids overkill in this spacious twin room. The silk coverlets and simple drapes have been kept deliberately muted to prevent the decor becoming too heavy-handed.

PATTERN **POWER**

Inspiration meets practicality in a big way when it comes to the art of wall decoration. Forms of faux finishes include mural painting, stenciling, distressing, sponging or marbling; they all add texture, pattern and focus to a room.

The options are plentiful: Bring style to a statement wall with gorgeous motifs or create character by tiling from floor to ceiling. Add prints, either within or without frames, in blocks of even numbers. Alternatively, use graphics in the form of transfers or stencils to bring life and color behind a bed. Naturally, wallpaper is another option: the current hot trend is for paper from managed timber sources printed with water-based inks; the ethos is eco-friendly and the look up-to-the-minute.

Relatively easy to achieve, stencil patterns can be highly dramatic — especially in the bedroom. Used extensively in the visual arts, the technique involves reproducing designs by passing ink or paint over holes cut in cardboard or metal. Homemade or bought stencils may be used for a variety of effects: creating columns, vertical or horizontal borders, one-off patterns or, indeed, whole walls. If you try stenciling at home, use a professional stenciling brush with short, stiff bristles and employ quick up-and-down movements to dab the paint on the wall, thereby preventing paint getting under the edges of the stencil. Start painting on the edges of the stencil, then work into the center, and adhere to the adage of less is more. Two thin coats give a better result than one thicker one.

Full-height feature walls can also be built to conceal storage. As long as they stretch from floor to ceiling, the possibilities are endless. Access may be through sliding or hidden doors and the space behind may be as big or as small as you wish. Many people opt for walk-in wardrobes behind such decorative "walls".

Our selection showcases some sumptuous bedrooms, all ameloriated by bold detailing: there's a touch of the Midas about the gold stencils inspired by Thai florals, while the bold colors at Singapore's Naumi hotel boost any guest's mood. Other rooms feature sponging, bold wallpaper and rolls of thick fabric. Because of this rich patterning, we advise restraint when it comes to bed linen choice.

Above A retro feeling is evoked in this subdued bedroom with the use of faux-antique sponging in a golden hue on the walls. Designer Kathleen Henares was briefed to produce something that harked back to the '50s: the beaded lampshade and deco-style headboard helps her here.

Right Bold colors and whimsical shapes characterise this ornamental installation that creeps up the walls of both bar and bedrooms at Singapore's upscale Naumi hotel. Designed by eco-id design consultancy, the three-layered sculpture features a mirror backing, flowers, frogs and butterflies cut from thin steel, and a huge glass sheet. Moreover, it changes color — from lavender to purple, ocean blue to fuchsia — depending on the time of the day. Above the bed, it truly heightens the senses.

Above The super-decadent home of Filipino designer Anton R Mendoza is an over-the-top combination of opulent materials and high quality art and antiques. The boho-chic master bedroom sports an extraordinary antique French bed that stands before a brocade-covered wallboard from England. The power dressing continues with a pair of Kartell lamps on antique night stands.
Above right The art of *pochoir* (French for stencil) is a refined stencil printing process that was used by Picasso and Miro. Here, the stencilled wall sports a border at its base and ceiling line, as well as repeated patterns elsewhere.
Right Known in China as early as the 8th century and apparently perfected by Eskimos before their contact with Westerners, stenciling is used today in Pop-art paintings and mimeographs as well as in interior design. Here, a stencilled border separates wallpaper from paint at hip level.

RUNNING COMMENTARY

In recent years runners for both beds and tables have experienced a resurgence in popularity, not least because they add color, theatricality and drama to a room at a relatively modest cost. Furthermore, in the tropics, they are frequently made from remnants of old textiles such as fragments from a kimono or hand-woven antique cloth, thereby anchoring the room with a definitive taste of Asia. In Thailand, the use of hill tribe textiles in decorative schemes is quite common: bed runners, cushions, pillows and throws are all suitable for such textile re-use. Of particular note is the cross-stitch of the Karen in their distinctive pink and blue shades; the intricate embroidery of the Hmong; and the slightly faded blue-jean look of the fabric of the Yao. Each tribe has its own culture of weaving patterns and all are rich in significance.

In order to preserve their ancient craft, a number of companies work with hill-tribe weavers to reproduce their original patterns in exciting and experimental ways. Because of the rich detailing, these work best in modern homes as accent rather than complete vernacular. Fabrics run the gamut from fine silks and a mix of cotton and silk with gold thread to rough and medium-weight homespun cotton, as well as hemp, flax and jute.

In Japan, traditionally, no part of a silk kimono was ever wasted, so it was a logical step for pieces from vintage kimono to find new life as home accents. Similarly, Indian saris and sarongs make for bright, colorful runners. And in the Philippines, *abaca* or Manila hemp, produced from the fibers of *Musa textiles*, a species of banana, gives a semi-transparent, shimmery effect on a bed.

There's no doubt that such runners are multi-faceted and full of character. Added to their beauty is the plus point that many of their hand-woven patterns tell a story or have an in-built history. For bed-time reading, what could be more beguiling?

Above left Polished teak, custom-made upholstery from Jim Thompson, a Persian carpet, and a runner in a Thai ethnic weave give this bedroom a luxurious feel.

Above Richly-colored Thai and Lao textiles have been taken from a *phaa sin* or long wraparound skirt and re-used here on the canopy border, runner and scatter cushions of this attractive bed. The use of white cotton in both sheets and drapes lightens the scenario.

Far left A fresh color palette characterises this spacious bedroom in Chiang Mai where designer Cindi Novcov has paired a futon, with dual runners, on the floor with a textured Berber wool carpet.

Middle left This villa bedroom is characterised by recycled materials: the cushions and runner, the gable and eave decorations on wall and console, and adapted lampstands.

Left A bright pink and purple cotton sarong throw adds a cheerful accent to this spacious villa bedroom at Mandala Resort in Boracay.

SLEEPING IN THE TROPICS

LUXE LOUNGING

Having an area in the bedroom reserved for lounging is no longer a luxury: for many it's a necessity. The desire for a private space — for reading or quiet contemplation away from the hustle and bustle of the rest of the home — is a very real need.

Asia provides a multitude of ideas for such a space: a colonial chaise lounge or pair of planter's chairs, for example; a deep sink-in sofa upholstered with tribal fabrics; a reconditioned day bed with a plethora of scatter cushions; a small desk and chair for those less inclined to recline. Alternatively, many opt to dress the bed as a lounger during the day: this can be achieved by adding back cushions, somewhere to store books or writing materials (try a low *khantoke* tray, a type of pedestal table that sits easily on the bed; they're available everywhere in Thailand), and some intimate lighting.

There's an abundance of materials for such nooks. A bamboo lounger and footrest looks suitably tropical when accompanied by homespun cotton cushions. Using bamboo is not only practical as it far outperforms most other woods in terms of durability, it's environmentally friendly too. Bamboo is usually harvested from monitored forests and re-grows in three to five years (unlike hardwood alternatives that take 15 to 25 years), so you can rest easy regarding your environmental footprint when using it.

Try to give the area its own identity away from the rest of the bedroom. This may be achieved with a different paint finish, a couple of choice artifacts, a different mood in the lighting, or by separating it from the bed with a large rug or bookcase. Personalizing it with precious mementoes can be fun too: it's up to you how far you go in this department.

Top far left In a bedroom that is a bit short on space, you may have to opt for a simple chair and footstool. This local rattan duo is perfectly acceptable.
Top middle More spacious rooms can often accommodate an entire living room scenario. Note the large pillar that helps separate the two areas.
Top right A small in-built bench in a niche offers extra space for privacy away from the bed, yet the two areas are united by the olive green color scheme in cushions, runner and lamp.

Above left Placing an intriguing piece of furniture in the bedroom at an angle adds a focal point away from the bed. This fresh chaise longue, a Western form, is an inspired idea in a room dominated by northern Thai furniture and artifacts.
Above right If it weren't for the Thai silk bed cover and ruched detailing in salmon pink above the bed, this bedroom could very well come from an English country home. The two plump armchairs and footstool are formally arranged away from the bed with helpful reading lamps behind.

Left French-style delicate lacework displayed on an antique metal four poster and bedside table in the Kanh family home in Ho Chi Minh city. White and cream are not the only colors used in modern Vietnamese embroidery: bright silks and velvets in reds and pinks are popular too today.

Right Goa was another colony where European, in this case Portuguese, influence is evident in furniture, architecture and art. This old Indo-Portuguese villa with its cavernous rooms, original tiled floors and period detailing is home to many original pieces. The heavy intricately carved four poster bed sports typical Portuguese-style crochet work.

DELICATE EMBROIDERY, APPLIQUÉ, CROCHET AND LACE

Dreamy, romantic and delicately detailed, white bed linen that employs hand-sewn or hand-woven virtuosity has a rich history in Asia. Predominant in countries with a colonial past, techniques are time-consuming and intricate, but the result is wares of a very high quality.

In the Philippines during the Spanish colonial period, the art of embroidery was part of the school curriculum, so Hispanized communities developed a number of different styles. *Calado* or piercing involved pulling out fibers from certain areas of a piece of cloth and strengthening the other areas with intricate floral and vegetal patterns. *Sombrado* was a type of appliqué in curvilinear patterns, while crocheting and straightforward embroidery were used extensively in the home.

Embroidered paintings and other works were common in Vietnam from the 17th century onwards, with a certain Lê Công Thành credited with introducing the art of embroidery to the country after a diplomatic trip to China. With the advent of colonialism, the ancient craft expanded significantly when the wives of French officials hired Vietnamese women to help with their dressmaking. By the end of the 19th century a new class of urban artisans skilled in French-style lace embroidery known as *cô khâu đầm* (sewing ladies) emerged in urban centers; their workshops expanded over time and lace for export became much sought after. By the 1930s the northern province of Hà Đông alone had some 4,000 lacemakers! Even today, the country is famous throughout Asia for its embroidered wares.

Another community who produced highly embellished embroidered and beaded works was that of the Malay-Chinese Peranakan. In the past, young Peranakan women (*nyonyas*) were judged by the quality of their sewing and were expected to have perfected the art of cross-stitch, beading and embroidery before they were of marriageable age. Today, the art has all but died out and it is difficult to find Peranakan work outside museums.

Examples of all these communities' skills are displayed on these pages. Particularly suited to the bedroom, such delicate work creates an aesthetic both nostalgic and magical; it's as if a bygone era has been resurrected along with the bed linen, drapes, sconces and swatches.

Top A museum in Singapore showcasing the fusion culture of the region's Peranakans gives a fascinating insight into the domestic habits of this highly skilled community. Here, displayed on a bed taken from an original Peranakan household, is some exceptionally fine, antique hand-embroidered linen.

Above Antique mosquito net hooks rest on a delicate mat embroidered with a floral motif.

Far left A bedroom in the neo-Classical Manila Hotel (built in the American-era in 1912, extensively restored in 1975) is decorated in Spanish-Filipino style evoking a former era of luxury and elegance.

Left A contemporary bedroom in the Philippines features sweetly embroidered Indian silk backboard and cushion with quilted bed coverings in Jim Thompson silk.

SLEEPING IN THE TROPICS

Above left Chiang Mai's Rachamankha hotel is an inspired combo of northern Thai architecture and the linked courtyard style of Chinese *siheyuan* buildings. Fittingly, it houses a mix of Lanna and Chinese antique furniture and artworks, as evidenced in this elegant bedroom where Chinese scrolls and a wedding cabinet mix with a simple Thai platform bed. The custom-crafted lantern takes influences from Thai temple lamp design, but has a Chinese touch in its hanging tassel.

Above right Chinese elements in this bedroom include the bamboo bed's red-and-gold dragon canopy, a Chinese latticed door and an auspicious Chinese character wooden tablet. The textiles on the bed and chair are from Studio Naenna, a company in Chiang Mai that specializes in preserving Lanna woven works in natural dyes.

Right Details from a Chinese-style bedroom include red-and-gold wallpaper, red velvet upholstery and low-level rosewood table with mother-of-pearl floral insets.

Middle right and far right The bridal chamber of a Peranakan household symbolized the status and wealth of the family: here, a namwood bed, lacquered in red and heavily gilded, is decorated with heavy silks embroidered with auspicious motifs.

CHINESE NIGHTS

As night falls over the tropical household, the Asian sky with its blanket of stars shines through many a bedroom window. Chances are that plenty of the inhabitants sleeping therein will be ensconced in a Chinese-inspired room, perhaps snuggled up in an elaborate Chinese four-poster bed.

Somehow, Chinese décor — be it Oriental opulent or Ming minimalist — is well suited to this most private of spaces. Exuberant colorful silks with minutely detailed hand-embroidery, the clean, contemporary lines of Ming dynasty furniture, Chinese lanterns and chinoiserie-style wallpaper, old opium loungers . . . all produce a vocabulary of design that soothes the soul for a restful night's sleep.

Our selection comes from a number of different Chinese sources: from China itself, from the Peranakan community in Singapore, and from Thailand where Chinese influences are particularly strong. Lacquered Chinese wedding cabinets always look stunning in a master bedroom as either an entertainment center or an armoire for storing clothing or linens. Similarly, other furniture items such as the low-level *tang* can double up as a bed or table; when made from rosewood with mother-of-pearl inlay, they are especially impressive. We're particularly keen on the Chinese penchant for black and red in a room scheme: it adds a bordello feel to the boudoir.

The Peranakans or Straits-born Chinese (see previous pages) evolved a very particular type of culture, assimilating some customs from the lands they settled in whilst maintaining many Chinese traditions. In addition to being expert cooks, the women or *nyonyas* were dab hands at embroidery and hand beading and, even though these skills are fast dying out, there remain in Asia a number of their works. Take a look at the lush drapes and covers on our elaborately carved Chinese day bed (left); they would have been reserved for the marriage suite.

Whether it's a touch of classical Chinese design you require or a full-on lavish lashing of vibrant color and carving, the term "Made in China" is no longer reserved for cheap and cheerful. Today, more often than not, it signifies a vibrant reinterpretation of ancient Chinese forms in a thoroughly modern idiom.

DINING IN
THE TROPICS

Dining in the tropics tends toward the casual, al fresco affair — with many homes not having a particular room dedicated entirely to dining. As such, fun and flexibility are the name of the game. Go for multi-functional spaces and items of furniture that lend themselves to adaptive reuse: The table you use for dinner turns into a desk between meals, your multi-purpose verandah works both as a lunch venue and an office.

We advise keeping the "room" and its contents low key. Go for a super-long but simple wooden table and add a set of white chairs to keep the look fresh and modern. The table acts as a bridge between work and play; seating can be set up at one end for a quick meal, at the other for a mini office with laptop. Hard-wearing wood is practical, but if you want to enlarge the space you may want to consider glass or Perspex.

Traditionally, most Asian homes did not have much in the way of furniture, so eating, drinking and lounging (as well as sleeping) took place on the floor. We're seeing many contemporary home owners following suit (see left), so we've come up with a bunch of ideas for low-level entertaining. You may find a slab of wood on breeze blocks surrounded by a bunch of poufs and cushions ticks your boxes. It's space saving too.

Whatever your taste, the key is to appear as if you haven't tried too hard. Eschew formality for a trestle table in the garden, a round table with a lazy susan on the verandah, or a semi open-plan area adjacent the kitchen. Bring color into the equation, with bright chairs and ceramics, and mis-matched glasses and plates. The following pages are full of innovative ideas for tables and chairs, table settings, floral decoration and more. And if you do want to give a no-holds-barred up-market dinner party, we show you how to do it — tropical-style.

Even though this dining room is fully enclosed, it has a light, breezy air because of its cool sage green color scheme. A rustic low table and mat, nature-themed art pieces in wall niches, a traditional rice paddy hat doubling up as a lightshade — all elements combine to produce a relaxed, fuss free ensemble. Owner Anneke van Waesberghe calls her style "nomadic chic" and certainly this room could be cleared very quickly and changed into something entirely different in minutes.

TROPICAL MODERN

Much of the design coming out of Asia these days eschews a penchant for intricacy with a cleaner-lined, more modern aesthetic. Heavy wood carving and rich embellishment largely remain in the area of antiques; contemporary works seem to favor simplicity, albeit a simplicity that is deceptively sophisticated.

Trend watchers note that trend-setters, especially in the dining domain, often hail from Japan. Restaurant design firms, Super Potato, SPIN Design Studio and Design Spirits, all Tokyo based, are responsible for some of the most stunning f&b outlets in the world. Their designs favor concepts such as harmony, balance and elegance, all the while heralding texture and geometry. The origins may hark back to the ritualistic tea ceremony, the raked Zen garden, the folds of a kimono, the *shoji* screen — but the works are firmly rooted in the here and now.

As far as dining rooms go, such firms often take used or salvaged materials to add depth into a design. They'll focus on layers of meaning, fine-tune the lighting and keep the actual table and chairs streamlined and simple. There may be an ethnic element, but it will be cloaked by an international neo-minimalist aesthetic.

Our dining choices illustrate this move towards quality, tactility and versatility. Table forms may be mainly traditional in shape, but materials are distinctive. The same goes for the table settings: Designs are global, materials local. Where you may see some flamboyance is in the floral decoration; here, sculptural shapes dominate, but color, variety and pattern are all impotant too.

Left No longer banished outdoors, this simple arrangement from Pattaya Furniture Collection illustrates how tropical rattan and coconut wood can be streamlined for indoor furniture use. The high backed chairs are comfy (rattan breathes, so they're well suited to the climate), but can also easily serve as office chairs when the glass-topped table turns into a typing pool.

Above At the Dumancas family home in Manila, cotton covers with whimsical tassels are practical and protective on dining chairs. The overall look is sober and elegant, enhanced by a row of antique celadon jars from China.

Above right A Joey Yupangco interior in Manila features a clean-lined dining space with classic white-and-chrome table designed by Patricia Urquiola and leather "Dart" chairs by Hannes Wettstein. The vases on table and console are by prominent Czech architect and designer Borek Sipek, known for his individual neo-baroque work.

Right A custom-crafted onyx and steel dining table is cleverly lit from below, an effect that is dramatised by a wood-paneled wall and dark chair backs. The wow factor is furthered with a rich red Villeroy & Boch dining service and elegant, long-stemmed glasses from Club 21.

Left Dark wood and mats contrast beautifully with square white ceramic plates and olive green bowls in the home of Filipino designer Lor Calma.
Below Filipino designer, Antonio Layug, is known throughout the tropical world for his organically inspired furniture and furnishings. Selling both locally and internationally, he has been hugely instrumental in bringing furniture design and manufacturing from the Phillipines to world attention. Here, a slightly curved hardwood table is matched with finely woven, yet extremely durable, polyethylene rattan chairs; the table was purposely angled to mimic the shape of the staircase behind.

Left A lively centerpiece is the focus on this dark-stained dining table. Coconut fronds have been carefully looped beneath the hanging petals of the spider lily, then placed in lengths of banana tree trunk. The idea behind the arrangement, explains florist Sakul Intakul, was to make the spider lilies appear to dance.
Below A massive *dao* wood table is dressed in artful natural style for dinner; seating 12 comfortably, it doubles up as a work space as well.
Bottom left A simple glass table with dressed chairs features nature-inspired plates, irridescent shell side plates and a slightly messy jug with flowers for an informal feel.
Bottom right Filipino restaurateur, Rikki Dee, has a passion for design, so when it came to designing a new home, he made many hands-on decisions. The dining room features a glass topped table, heavy *kamagong* sideboard and black glass sliding doors; when not in use, it is decorated with a mix of fruit, leaves and flowers.

INDIGO NIGHTS

Evening dining on an airy verandah or deck, preferably with gorgeous views of ocean and the night sky, can be extremely evocative in the tropics. Not only has the heat of the day subsided by nightfall, the flicker of candlelight, the sounds of crickets and frogs and, hopefully, the lapping of waves or gurgling from an adjacent water feature all contribute to an atmospheric alfresco experience.

For maximum comfort, we recommend cane or rattan chairs with cushions as these allow for adequate air circulation, but as long as the chairs aren't placed too close to their neighbor, other types will do. Tables should be dressed simply and lighting restricted to citronella tea lights (good to deter bugs). Lighting "borrowed" from the house, or from the garden and pool, should provide enough in the way of other ambient light.

At dusk, tropical night skies take on an indigo hue (what photographers term the "blue hour") that lasts 20 minutes or so. The ethereal light at this time is the effect you want to try to capture. If not *en plein air*, hang low-level pendant lamps with blue light bulbs on a low wattage above the table; the effect can be quite realistic. Another option is to use battery operated table lamps with deep blue shades; not only do these dispense with ugly wires, they cast an attractive hue over any table.

Yet another alternative is to get creative with a floral centerpiece: floating lotus blossoms crowned with lit candles in a shallow dish filled with water are tranquil and tropical; or try something more sculptural in a row of identical glass vases.

Above A couple of spotlights and borrowed light from the hanging lantern in the adjacent gateway (partially seen) provide all the illumination needed for this inviting dining scene. The tranquil ornamental pond catches the reflection of the white-washed pillars and provides a cooling element.

Above right A large urn with floating candles adds atmosphere to this fine dining scene, but most of the actual illumination comes from the custom-crafted steel chandelier designed by Yasuhiro Koichi. The sound of water is ever present, as the textured wall in the background houses a water cascade.

Right Underwater lighting from this villa's amoeba-shaped pool provides ample illumination for this meal beneath the stars. A simple melamine table and boxy chaises are all that's necessary.

Far left A small balcony hosts a dinner for two. A tatami mat on a simple table, flanked by Natuzzi chairs, sits aside a versatile, chrome-clad console table and modern "tree", both by architect and jewelry designer Ana Rocha.

Left *Bai-sri* and *bencharong* are fine dining partners for Bangkok's skyline at night.

LOW LEVEL **DINING**

Traditionally, in most Asian societies, life within the home was lived on the floor. This was partly because furniture was rare, and when it existed at all was low, and partly because of hierarchy in societal structures. Thrones and chairs were reserved for religious leaders and rulers; ordinary mortals sat on the floor.

Similarly, there was no particular room that was set aside for dining. People tended to use the verandah or a communal room to eat in. A cloth or banana leaf was simply laid out on the rush matting on the floor — and the meal commenced.

With Westernisation came Western customs including the practice of sitting on chairs and dining at tables. Yet, even today, many people prefer to follow ancient traditions and continue to dine in the time-honored manner — at a low level.

We showcase some examples from around the region: on a verandah in Thailand, in private homes in Singapore and Bali, and in two restaurants in Malaysia and Thailand. The Thai triangular cushion or *maun kwan*, densely packed with kapok, is particularly suited to such a well-grounded scenario. It inclines at just the right angle to support the side when sitting, and sometimes comes with the addition of a folding mattress for extra comfort.

Right A wild jungle setting in Malaysia provides a suitably tropical backdrop for this casual, somewhat rustic, low-level dining scene.
Middle right Red-lacquered *khantoke* trays placed on low tables provide a delightful Thai accent in this al fresco setting overlooking a lily pond. Ceramic bowls with insides glazed with celadon, outsides unglazed, are perfect for spicy soups. From Mae Rim Ceramics, Chiang Mai.

Far right A formal feel is achieved here with high-quality silk fabrics, exquisite Thai *bencharong* dinner service, blush pink lotus arrangements and low lighting. The burnished teak panels and highly polished low *tang* tables contribute too.

Above left Doors and windows have been dispensed with in the dining area of an apartment in Singapore. This radical step allows for cooling by cross breezes and a nature-inspired atmosphere. "The idea was a throwback to tropical living before the advent of that dreaded 20th century invention — the air conditioner," explains Karina Zabihi of kzdesigns. In keeping with the light airy feel is the eggshell blue color scheme, delicate cushions and see through Perspex table.

Above right Designed by Ed Tuttle, this teak pavilion houses a wonderful circular low table with attendant wood carving and triangular floor cushions.

Above An imposing room with high ceilings, along with antique furniture and light fittings, certainly helps when it comes to arranging a chic tropical table. This home in Vietnam has the architecture; it is complemented by a beautifully appliquéed Vietnamese linen tablecloth, antique etched glass candle holders and a lacquerware dinner set.

Left Sterling silver, cut crystal and rich porcelain make fine dining partners at the Manila hotel.

Right A super long table arranged with high backed chairs upholstered in silk makes an elegant statement at the Jim Thompson restaurant in Singapore.

Middle right Designed to replicate an elaborate setting in Burma during the colonial period, this dining room is a fanciful mix of glossy surfaces and gold decoration.

Far right 17th century blue-and-white Chinese porcelain and fluted glasses grace the table at the Jim Thompson house. Thompson was famous for his entertaining — but apparently the food at his table was terrible!

A TASTE OF **TRADITION**

Sometimes, when the mood takes us, we turn to tradition, rigor and good, old-fashioned formality in the dining room. More often than not, this is to be had in an elegant restaurant setting, with fine wining and dining, silver service, starched tablecloths and hovering waiters. However, it is possible to create a highly formal dining room at home.

Key ingredients for such a dinner party include highly stylized floral decoration, elegant crystal glasses and decanters, exquisite china and seductive lighting. A long wooden table with stiff-backed chairs placed beneath a chandelier sets the scene; it should be candle lit, preferably with arching sterling silver candelabra. Ideally, flatware, napkins and mats should be antique: Delicate decadence may be achieved with lacy, hand-embroidered mats from the Philippines, and, for an Asian feel, experiment with *bencharong* porcelain, made in China from Thai designs, or blue-and-white wares from the Ming period.

An exotic mood can be achieved through the Thai art of flower arranging, a skill that has been taught to Thai noblewomen since the Sukhothai period. Be it a bouquet, a garland, a type of floral lace or a sculptural form, the idea is to rearrange or modify flowers so that they reappear in new forms, different from their natural states. Intricate and delicate, such designs make for artistic centerpieces. Another option is the craft of *bai-sri*, whereby folded banana leaves and floral arrangements traditionally used for religious offerings, grace the table. The time-honored art of *kai sa luk* or fruit and vegetable carving, whereby the mundane is transformed into the magical, is another traditional form of decoration in Thailand. Melons reworked into multi-petalled flowers are just one example — they make for fruity topics of conversation.

Visit some of Asia's neo-Classical heritage hotels to get other ideas for fine dining. The Tiffin Room in Raffles hotel boasts some extraordinary floral arrangements, while Bangkok's Oriental hotel has a beautifully presented afternoon tea service. The high-vaulted dining rooms of such colonial strongholds still stick to tradition: formal settings, sumptuous food and highly personalized service.

Above When the owner of this Ayutthyan home had it reassembled in Bangkok, he adhered to traditional forms but also adapted the building to contemporary living. Breaking with tradition, he placed the formal dining room atop the *chan-ban* platform and furnished it with classic Thai-style teak furniture and artifacts. The two ceremonial spirit paintings form the Yao hill tribe in northern Laos are imposing as are the antique display cabinets with a fine collection of Thai ceramics. **Left** Thai-style table decoration in the form of sculptural jasmine blooms are fresh and elegant.

Right The owner of this palatial home in Yangon (Rangoon) is an avid collector of Southeast Asian ceramics, many of which were made in the UK and the Netherlands to Asian specifications and exported to the region in the 19th and 20th centuries. They make for an individual display in a formal dining room, the centerpiece of which is an oval table made of unpolished metal sheet. When the custom-crafted chandelier, based on the design of a temple *hti* or umbrella, is lit, flickering candles are reflected in its smooth surface below.

DINING IN THE TROPICS

THE GREAT
OUTDOORS

Al fresco, verandah or garden dining can incorporate any number of styles and settings. Our preference for simple food and rustic presentation can be cast aside if, for example, it's a wedding banquet you're organizing. On these pages, we showcase a variety of outdoor dining options, from the super elaborate to the homey and informal.

One thing is a constant though: floral decoration. Again, depending on the type of look you want to achieve, it can be as simple as a couple of sculptural leaves in a glass jar or as intricate as a multi-tiered ensemble of choice blooms. Whatever you opt for, be sure to keep the arrangements inside in the cool until the last minute; wilted flowers in hot sunshine look very sad.

Water is always a cooling element, and tropical days frequently need cooling down. If you don't have a river, ocean or *klong* handy, the next best thing is a swimming pool or water feature. Simply looking at water or listening to the soothing sounds of water brings the temperature down. Similarly, opt for cold soups, big jugs of iced juices, light salads and the like; heavy foods don't have a place in the great outdoors.

Asia is home to numerous artisans molding, sculpting and firing a huge range of ceramics, so there's no excuse for shoddy tableware. Our recommendations include the delicate hues of cracked celadon, fresh blue-and-white, and clean white in modern shapes. Napkins and cloths should be textured and soft, preferably in bright, cheerful colors.

Left top Chiang Mai's Gong Dee gallery prides itself on producing a range of goods that has revitalised Lanna craftsmanship. Contrary to its usual style, this table and chairs bear European design influences combining glass and wood with a synthetic material developed to resemble roughly-hewn stone. The hardness of the "stone" contrasts with the soft upholstery and wooden arms and legs — and looks very distinctive in an outdoor setting.

Above A romantic set up adjacent the Indian ocean in Bali with a dressed table and elaborate floral centerpiece is fit for a king and queen. Pale blue-green recyled glass plates and glasses are suitable for a fresh outdoors look, while the green silk runner connects the table with the lawn on which it is placed. The crème de la crème of the ensemble, however, is the pair of flags usually found outside Balinese temples: here they take on a white flowing form fluttering in the breeze.

Right Dusk on a deck overlooking the Irrawaddy river must be prime time to dine in Bagan (Pagan). Plain dishcloth cotton is used for napkins and cloths, while rice and prawn crackers are served in lacquerware bowl and plates.

Opposite bottom A table and chairs manufactured in the Philippines by French company Sifas is made from a type of synthetic rattan that does not fade, warp, fray or bleach, even if left outdoors for long periods. As such it is highly suited for tropical outdoor dining, as is the fresh green color of the chair cushions.

TROPICAL TABLES,
CASUAL DINING

For the most part, tropical dining is a casual affair. Many homes don't even have a formal dining room, with dining tables often placed adjacent the kitchen or on the verandah. Where there is a special room, you'll often find it has a multi-functional purpose: it can double up as a place to work from as well as to entertain in.

As such, tables need to be flexible: bespoke, super-long models are highly practical, while the trestle table is easily dismantled and stored when not in use. Folding tables are another alternative. If the table is placed near an open-plan kitchen, the area turns into a social center too: the chef can converse with guests while cooking.

Ubiquitous wood is an obvious choice in the tropics. Be it stained a dark mahogany or a lighter shade, it adds warmth to a room. If teamed with white chairs or a bench with white cushions, the look will be fresh and natural. White tableware in organic shapes looks appealing with all tones of wood, too.

If you want to enlarge your dining room, a see-through glass table is a good choice. Glass is increasingly the material of choice for much furniture around the home, as it creates the illusion of more space. An airy arrangement of glass-topped table and an eclectic mix of chairs is a top choice for a small space; it doesn't block out light and can look very modern.

Left top For an outdoor setting, a low-ish table set beneath an umbrella with comfy sofa and lounge chair seating is ideal. Shades of vermilion and orange are suitably tropical, with grey a useful neutral.
Left middle Lacquered table and bench top furniture with stainless steel legs is designed in Vietnam by Quasar Khanh. Khanh was attracted to stainless steel as it is very light; hence, such furniture is easily transported from one part of the house to another.
Left bottom A colonial-style setting with polished wood table and cane-and-wood chairs is a timeless classic. The artwork is by Goa-based sculptor and painter Subodh Kerkar.

Above A bright, airy effect is achieved here with the use of glass, water and light that enters via this shophouse airwell. Adding to the cheerful composition is a simple table with bright toned floral arrangement and earth-toned ceramic tableware. The curved wooden chairs are from Space; note how their wood tone mimics that of the door handles.
Left This deceptively simple small dining room is a study in carefully thought through design details. Wooden slatted walls are painted white and paired with breezy sari curtains in a light beige shade, thereby enlarging the space. The table's statement-making color is offset by fine high-backed chairs with a leather finish and tableware that sports a delicate crackled glaze. Cute individual purple vanda blooms "wrapped" in *Calathea* leaves are matched by the pastel hue of light mauve napkins.

Left The casual covered verandah in this home in the Philippines is a picture of light, airy elegance. The dark stained wooden table comfortably seats six on light rattan chairs. **Below** A rustic Balinese home built entirely from teak has a large open space that doubles up as both dining and living area. Surrounded by assorted statuary, a long trestle table is set for lunch with pastel-toned tableware from Jenggala Keramik.

Above Somewhat messy, but cheerful and homey, a long slim table displays a selection of Thai lacquerware food containers. The mismatched chairs add to the general laissez faire feeling.

Above right Thai green celadon coffee table and containers sit before a casual dining area on the verandah of a Thai home. A trellis above casts shade; in fact, the area can be closed off with heavy wooden shutters if so required.

Right An ironwood deck protected by a Plexiglass roof plays host to a casual table with revolving chairs in a Sarawak home. The surrounding garden is a riot of orchids, ferns and anthuriums; at night, illumination comes courtesy of a pendant light encased in a fish trap shade.

From left to right Modern lacquerware plate and box from Myanmar made in the traditional manner. Boxes, bowls and vase with intricate floral design from Lanna artisans. An illuminated tabletop in onyx is a suitably exotic backdrop for this Villeroy & Boch tableware. Extremely rare, antique pumpkin-style boxes in green lacquer from the Shan State. The introduction of new pigments into Vietnamese lacquer has resulted in modern wares with bright, sometimes even acid, colors.

LACQUER WARES: **PAST AND PRESENT**

The art of lacquerware, whereby layers of natural lacquer resin are applied over bamboo- or wood-lattice, paper or pottery frames, then sanded, dried and re-applied multiple times to create enduring wares, is believed to have developed in 4th-century China. Be that as it may, contemporary items produced through the same time-honored methods are as beloved as those from the past.

Different types of wares evolved in different parts of the tropical world. In Japan, lacquer was used in paintings, prints, and on a wide variety of objects from Buddha statues to bento boxes. In Thailand, it was popular for multi-level betel bowls and Buddhist monks' offering bowls, as well as on paintings on walls and pillars in temples. Burmese lacquer wares are amongst the finest anywhere: ceremonial objects often bore intricate patterns, created by incising the multi-colored lacquer layers, but even utilitarian utensils are often exceptionally beautiful.

Vietnam is another country with a rich lacquerware history. Originally found only in red, black and green colors, lacquer was often used on larger pieces, such as chests and tables. Large ornamental screens showing Chinese influence with Asian scenes are particularly note-worthy. Today, lacquer wares come in any number of colors — the gold, silver and neon-colored trays, mats and bowls, seen in home décor shops all over the world, are more than likely manufactured in Hanoi.

We showcase some old styles, some new — and some in between! As each item can easily take up to six months to complete, these pieces are amongst the finest you'll see gracing an Asian home. Either practical or ornamental, they have an allure all their own.

Right Lacquerware from Myanmar's Shan State tends to comprise simple pieces with only one layer of red-dyed lacquer painted over one layer of black with no incising or gilding. These household objects are fairly utilitarian, yet attractive nonetheless; from the Claudia and Patrick Robert collection.

Right From the same collection, some fine 19th-century household items made to a Victorian design in the Chindwin District of Myanmar. The outer surfaces are black, the interiors red.
Left A Burmese stacked food container with multiple layers and lid is deceptively simple in two colors.

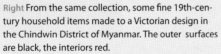

CONTEMPORARY
CERAMICS

Ceramic making and trading has a long history in Asia, with many countries — from India to South East Asia to China and Japan — producing ceramic wares of an exceptionally high quality from very early times. Earthenware and stoneware ceramics from Thailand and Indonesia, as well as blue-and-white porcelain from China and Japan, were amongst the earliest examples; these were followed by different techniques and styles, such as crackled-glaze finishes in celadon and the art of colorful *bencharong*, for example.

Contemporary ceramics, in large part, continue in their forebears' footsteps. Modern ateliers still hand-throw and kiln-fire their wares, often mimicking the strong earthy styles and colors of the past, but updating the wares with different shapes and finishes. When combined with other Asian artifacts — lacquerware, metallics, glassware, hand-woven textiles — they make for imaginative table settings.

Take Earth & Fire, the Bangkok-based ceramics producer. Its design philosophy is to create wares that are contemporary, functional and oriental ("It's never enough that something looks good; it has to work as beautifully as it looks," says the founder). Most of its wares are based on the country style of past traditions, but it combines this aesthetic with Japanese techniques and styles to come up with fresh pieces.

Jenggala Keramik in Bali is another case in point. A major supplier to the famed island's hotels and resorts, it describes its work as "forms of whimsy, modern practicality and organic twists". One of their famous lines, the Bamboo Collection, takes the distinctive lines of bamboo poles and the shape of cups and jugs used for the Indonesian tradition of drinking *tuak* to create a fun fusion range of wares. The Pincuk line works on a similar vein: it takes the folded banana leaf as its principal design inspiration.

The variety of tropical ceramics, both in Asia and available globally through export, is nothing short of phenomenal. Take some tips from the selection here. When combined with tropical florals such as delicate orchids or spidery chrysanthemums, they can be most beguiling.

Above Celadon Green, a company in Vietnam, produces high quality celadon ceramics in a variety of styles. In general, the glaze is jade-like, although it is difficult to guage the exact color until firing is complete. These bowls are incised with a decorative swirl that would have been found on 15th-century designs made in north Vietnam in Chinese-run factories.

Above Traditional northern Thai celadon by AKA Chiang Mai comes in both modern and traditional shapes.

Left top Mimicking the country-style earthenware of the past, these ceramics come in strong earthy colors and chunky designs. By Bangkok-based Earth & Fire.

Left middle A Japanese aesthetic has been introduced into this northern Thai celadon ware designed by Ekarit Praditsuwana.

Left bottom Imported techniques and colors from Japan transform modern noodle bowls into highly individual crackled-glaze pieces. From Bangkok-based Cocoon.

Below Mengrai Kilns, in Chiang Mai, are known for their handmade stoneware that sports strong colors and an appealing reflective sheen. Different pigments in the glazes and different firing temperatures result in these up-to-the minute designs.

THE TROPICAL BATHROOM

Be it an outdoor Jacuzzi set in a deck or a fully-enclosed private space, we give you a plethora of ideas for tropical bathing in this chapter. Bring the outdoors in, give precedence to either sink or tub (not both), enlarge with mirrors, create a zen-like spa space — whatever takes your fancy, it's here.

Because it's the tropics we're talking about, the outdoors and outdoor elements feature prominently. Borrowing from some of the region's most talented spa and bathroom designers and decorators, many troppo home owners have incorporated courtyard bathrooms into their homes and villas. But the look is easily extended into enclosed bathrooms too: bring plants, natural materials such as rocks, bamboo, pebbles and the like, as well as plenty of light and air into this most private of spaces — and you can transform the dullest of rooms into a full-on bathing beauty.

Because of the boom in Asia's spa business, we're seeing a lot more variety in bathroom hardware these days. Utilitarian tubs in standard shapes are increasingly being replaced by innovative bathing options — entire walk-through wet rooms, stand-alone tubs with pressure jets, huge rain showers with their massive roses, for example. LED colored mood lighting is almost de rigeur nowadays, and floor and wall coverings increasingly imaginative. Think large format tiles with a textural finish and glistening metallic sheen or a subtly shimmering wall of tiny pearlescent mosaics; limestone is always stylish for flooring, and if you live in a colder climate, be sure to install under floor heating before laying floor tiles.

Cutting edge technology comes to the closet with digital showering a major trend. Electric showers are particularly cost efficient, with eco-settings and precise temperature controls and programmes. And if you have high water pressure, the aerated showerhead injects air into the water, thereby boosting performance without wasting water. Check out all these new ideas — and create a truly indulgent bathroom; it'll be modern and eco-sensitive too.

Eva Shivdasani, the creative director of this his and hers duo, has opted for raw materials and finishes to create a country-style washroom here. Mirrors, mounted on pillars, are bordered with roughly hewn wood, while walls sport an outdoor, whitewashed look. The glass counter top enhances the free-flowing space.

OUTDOOR **BATHING**

There's something incredibly liberating about luxuriating in an outdoor bathroom, with nature and the natural world close to hand. Obviously, a warm climate is a must for such an experience, as is a profusion of tropical foliage, plenty of natural organics around, and either a clear blue sky or a star-studded hemisphere above.

However, a simulacrum can be created within the confines of four walls, a floor and a ceiling if more than a dash of imagination is utilized. Our selection of outdoor bathrooms is — for the most part — very much outdoors (often in quite remote, wild places), but, with a careful use of props, they could be adapted within more conventional confines.

Take the use of natural stone, for example. In some cases, here, the bathrooms have been shaped around the contours of large boulders that were originally found on the house site. A similar look can be recreated at home with clever use of river stones, moss-encrusted walls and palms and ferns in concealed pots or planter boxes. Add some sculptural driftwood or a stand of miniature bamboo, a large rain shower and some crazy paving — and you can imagine your Balham semi a Balinese villa.

Seriously, though, if you get the elements right, the rest follows. And if you do live in the tropics, take some inspiration from this selection. Don't be too rigid: a slightly slapdash use of sand and stones, pebbles and plants gives the right outdoorsy feel. Don't be too particular with the placement of items; you want a wild jungle not a manicured park. Go for rounded contours, irregular shapes and overgrown foliage. Cracked tile mosaics are another idea: they'll help with cleanliness, but look some-what thrown together.

Left top Terrazzo is the perfect material for an outdoor tub, especially one that is fed from a roughly-hewn stone cascade. The textured quality of the "walls" conceals hidden lighting.

Above A polished wooden deck, rustic chick blinds and a surrounding tropical garden are all that's needed here for a true back-to-nature bathing experience. Scented rose petals add to the spa feel.

Right A zen-like space is created here with the clever use of natural rocks, bamboo walls, a lone frangipani tree and wooden decking. The crème de la crème, however, is the round tub. Made from cement with a bronze finish via a process known as cold forging, it is a highly original piece.

Opposite bottom A Japanese effect is created with the use of geometric wooden trellis work and large sunken tub in Villa Shasa, Koh Samui, Thailand. Of course, the sea views add an extra dimension! It's hardly surprising that water forms a focus here, as the villa's name translates as "holy water".

Above Even though this bathroom is found in a Singapore apartment and is fully enclosed, it has the feeling of the great outdoors because of the addition of a small adjacent balcony that doubles up as shower cubicle and garden. Add to that light streaming through floor-to-ceiling glass, beautiful veined marble and a Corbusier lounger and you have a modern, yet tropical, feel.

Left Who would imagine that a rustic verandah could be transformed into something quite so stylish? The Japanese wooden tub and water container are complemented by unfinished wood counter and large ladder towel rail. Bumpy walls, a thatch and bamboo roof and chick blinds complete the open-air feel.

Left Billowing soft muslin drapes, an adjacent garden and cool, turquoise stone create a disctinctly ethereal al fresco feel in this Balinese villa bathroom designed by Valentina Audrito. Rustic water ladles and bowl by Japanese glass artist Seiki Torige sit on the bath rim while water bubbles from concealed jets.

Below Arranged adjacent an atrium lightwell, this shophouse conversion bathroom benefits from sliding glass doors that allow for the inclusion of light and air. Large urns containing mini trees are reflected in the wide mirror thereby enlarging what is in fact quite a narrow space.

THE TROPICAL BATHROOM

Right An over-sized tub clad in marble is the centerpiece of this garden bathroom at Ayana Villa. Scented candles in super-large wooden stands provide atmosphere at night.
Below Homemade products, such as rock salts for cleansing and ground coconut for a skin scrub are naturally scented. Mix them up with some floral blooms and aromatherapy oils in the bathwater, and you'll begin to unwind.

THE SPA **AT HOME**

Spa designers insist that creating a comforting, luxurious spa environment isn't terribly difficult. A clean-lined, uncluttered look with few distractions is essential, as are harmonious music, lighting, textures and aromas. The idea is to keep distractions to a minimum, so that clients are able to truly switch off. Zen den or modern minimalist, this is the feeling they're aiming for.

For those who don't have the time, inclination or money to visit a spa, or simply want a bit of "me-time" at home, there is always the option of creating the spa at home. It can't really match the all-encompassing escape of a true spa, but — in our experience — it can certainly come close.

Transforming your bathroom into a spa can be a fun project. Bubbles, flower petals, aromatic candles, hopefully some peace and quiet, a choice of meditative music and some beautiful, all-natural, scented products are necessities. And — if you are really serious about turning your humble tub into a no holds barred rub-a-dub-dub experience — invest in a Jacuzzi. Whirlpools come in a variety of shapes, sizes and prices these days; some even have the option of underwater lighting to heighten the therapeutic benefits of the water jets.

Our selection, mostly found in private villas and homes throughout the Asian region, splash out on the Jacuzzi, then keep the rest of the décor relatively simple. Natural organics, such as wooden decking, plants, pebbles, simple stone carvings and candles complement the high-quality marble, corian and other composite tubs. To enjoy such an environment, all that's needed is a couple of hours with the phone switched off and the knowledge that nobody is going to drop by. Bliss!

Left An intricate black-and-gold lacquerware panel depicting typical Thai scenes forms a dramatic backdrop to this Jacuzzi tub set in a bathroom niche. The tub benefits from in-built LED lighting too.

Above Built to resemble a Balinese spa, this deck with drop-in Jacuzzi is to be found at Brilliant Resort in China! The keyhole shape is an attractive one, especially when set at an angle to the surrounding floor boards.

Below Coco Palm Bodu Hithi is a tranquil hideaway in the north Malé atoll in the Maldives. Recreate their bathroom spa look at home with pale creams, taupes and cool eggshell shades; the addition of pebbles at the Jacuzzi's base gives a natural touch.

RETRO **REFLECTIONS**

Bathrooms with very modern sanitary wares, fixtures and fittings can be considerably softened with the addition of an antique mirror, some old-fashioned receptacles (decorative perfume bottles, vintage silver cups, for example) or some flea-market finds such as a pair of old prints. Gilt or heavy wooden frames on mirrors give the room some gravitas, while elaborate scrolls or Venetian glass etching produce a 1930s glamor feel.

Asia is renowned for its decorative glasswork, with India and Myanmar probably leading the way in artistic rendering. Burmese temples are often decorated with intricate mosaics of tiny colored glass or mirror pieces fashioned into floral, vegetal or geometric motifs. Covering whole pillars or walls in this manner is not uncommon — and the resulting shimmering effect translates well into a domestic setting too.

In India, the art of arranging tiny glass fragments into patterned mosaics is called *thekri* work. Unique to the Mewar region in Rajasthan, molten glass is blown into circular balls using pipettes. Then cool, molten mercury and lead are poured into the balls, coating the concave sides, and they're left to cool again. The balls are then broken into pieces, shaped, and stuck with an adhesive mix of lime and marble powder onto surfaces in different patterns. Whether the pattern is a simple geometric one or something more elaborate, the effect is stunning especially when candle lit.

In bathrooms, *thekri* work can be especially atmospheric. Line an alcove with such a glass mosaic and place an aromatherapeutic tea light at its base. Alternatively, construct your own mirror with a *thekri* surround — and bring a bit of Mewari magic into the room. If it was good enough for Maharajahs in the past, it's more than adequate for mere mortals today.

Left Intricate carving, illuminated by overhead lighting, forms the focus of a pair of mirrors in Ayana Villa. Reflected in their surface are framed Balinese fabric remnants.

Above A strong classical Vietnamese feel is achieved in this traditional-style powder room. A pair of basins sits on repro red-and-gold lacquered Imperial style basin stands. The mirrors are antique as are the glazed Chinese-style ventilation air tiles above.

Above right Reminiscent of Yangon's Botataung pagoda, the walls and ceiling of this bathroom in Myanmar are covered with reflective mosaic mirrored tiles. The work was carried out by a team of craftsmen from Mandalay; known as *hman-si-shwe-cha*, the technique is traditionally used in temple ornamentation in both Mon and Burman temples.

Right Austerity is softened in this modern bathroom with the addition of a gilt, European-style mirror.

WHITE CERAMICS, WOOD ACCENTS

A pairing of warm-toned teak wood and cool white ceramics forms the basis of the decorative scheme in these bathrooms. In all cases, there's a stark contrast between the dark stain of the wood and the pristine white of the sanitary ware; and, in all cases, the overall effect is daring and dramatic.

Although some of our examples come from traditional Asian houses constructed entirely from wood, the actual walls don't have to be wooden. Paneling in recycled teak is not impossible, while a more practical — and sustainable — alternative would be a wood veneer or laminate. Another option would be to merely accent the room with certain wood pieces such as old railway sleepers or a piece of driftwood, for example.

Today's laminates have improved in leaps and bounds since they first came on the market more than a century ago. Made by bonding together two or more layers of wood material with an adhesive and other products such as paper, fabric, plastic or metal, laminates are formed in the presence of pressure so are very hard wearing. Recent technological advances have helped with the bonding of edges, so nowadays an almost seamless join is possible. If you want a bit more sophistication and are willing to spend more, a hardwood veneer could be just the ticket: these are thin slices of wood, bonded to another composite wood product like plywood or particleboard, so are more "natural" in appearance.

Whichever you opt for, the idea in such a bathroom is to bring out the warmth of the wood while relishing the cool texture and appearance of the sanitary ware. White marble, tiles, terrazzo and corian are all durable, practical materials for sinks, baths and floors. Try experimenting with different combinations for different looks. The odd wooden artifact, such as a Burmese *hsun-ok* or lacquered bowl, furthers the comforting organic feel.

Far left Teak panelling is lightened here with the addition of soft, sensuous chick blinds, an oversized tub and in-built ladder towel rail. Note how crisp white towels fit well in this decorative scheme.

Middle left A powder room in the home of General Emilio Aguinaldo, the first president of the Republic of the Philippines, is a mix of European-style ceramic tiles and *narra* wood panelling. The rest of the home is no less eclectic: expressing the character of the general, it is now a museum.

Left A suite at the Dhara Dhevi in Chiang Mai has a bathroom and small ante chamber decked out in northern Thai style. An imposing *hsun ok* sits adjacent a comfortable couch upholstered in Thai silk, while the veined marble sink stand was hand carved.

Above left Bangkok's Oriental hotel has taken the teak-and-sleek look to an artful conclusion with handsome retro-chic washbasin, sturdy polished wood furniture and cupboards with framed mirror insets. The overall look is strong and masculine.

Above right Northern Thai woodcarving on wash stand, mirror and open-plan cupboard plays an important role in the design of this spacious bath-room. Gauzy white drapes (seen in mirror) work well with white ceramics too.

LIQUID ASSETS

Vessel sinks, as opposed to more traditional pedestal or wall-mounted sinks, are true liquid assets. Not only are they funky and hip, they offer the most choice when it comes to materials, shapes, sizes and depths.

In its simplest form, the vessel sink is a free-standing sink that sits directly on a vanity, countertop or other piece of furniture. Occasionally, you may choose to mount it directly off the wall. Its versatility is only one of its strengths and there are many other reasons to choose a vessel sink: They come in many different shapes (bowls, squares, oblongs, asymmetrical styles) and can be made from glass, marble, vitreous china, stainless steel, bronze, natural stone, cast iron and more.

In the past, most designers advocated that the toilet, sink and tub belong to a matching set, but that's not the case any more. If you opt for a vessel sink, it allows for greater flexibility as it can be paired with other aspects of your décor. For example opaque glass works well with frosted glass shelves and semi see-through shower cubicles; natural stone can echo a frieze of river pebbles; a strong color can work with a particular shade or hue in your curtains or blinds. Give the sink some space — and make it the main focus of the bathroom.

The choice of faucet is also important as the tap needs to be long or arched enough to direct into the center of the sink, especially if you have a round vessel. If the water falls on the side, there is a real danger of splashing. There are plenty of taps that can be wall mounted; these often work best with the vessel sink.

And for those who are interested in provenance: the vessel sink is based on the age-old design of Chinese washbasins that were placed in houses before the advent of running water. As such, they have an added authenticity when used in the Asian home.

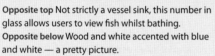

Opposite top Not strictly a vessel sink, this number in glass allows users to view fish whilst bathing.
Opposite below Wood and white accented with blue and white — a pretty picture.
Clockwise from above Frosted glass and corian; long vanity in shining white; quirky basin made from a kitchen wok; handbeaten metal sinks with oversized arching faucets; funky metal sink fashioned into glass shelving unit; two types of Thai travertine.

Right Textural surfaces are the key to the success of the overall look in this bathroom at the Farm at San Benito: Walls are fashioned from terrazzo inlaid with mother-of-pearl, the floor alternates between pebbles and natural granite tiles, the ceiling is a mélange of natural coconut tiles, and the crème de la crème of the whole — a vessel bowl sink fashioned from polyurethane resin.

Below Light and airy, this urban bathroom combines mirrors, marble, chrome and green tinted glass for an elegant, modern feel.

Opposite clockwise from top left Italian hardware in a Bangkok loft: A masculine effect is achieved with both the strong color scheme and the metal, glass and chrome sanitary ware. The owner of this batchelor pad harbors a love for Italian design, and it shows with this top-quality kit.

Lacquered surfaces, lotus flowers, a strong white ceramic sink and soft hand towels make for a dramatic powder room.

Extending a counter out of a natural boulder, then insetting a burnished vessel sink shows imagination in an outdoor bathroom in Koh Samui. Here, landscape really is part of the decorative scheme; it's interesting to see how vessel sinks can sink as well as rise.

Taking the rough with the smooth: A strong sculptural look is created with carved natural stone basin and dark wood vanity and splash-back. Recessed lighting behind the mirror softens the overall feel.

Above The texture of this sanded and carved Balinese door contrasts beautifully with soft limestone walls and the tub's polished surface at Ayana Villa. The tear-drop shape of the bath is a fairly new design; wider at one end than the other, it is specially designed for comfortable reclining.

THE SPACE AGE

Recent trends in bathroom design have included both the widening of the scope of the bathroom, and the widening of the room itself. More and more people see the bathroom as their own private comfort zone, a chill-out area where they won't be disturbed — and as such, it needs to be spacious enough to accommodate more than just tub, sink and toilet.

In America and Europe in the 1880s and 1890s, when bathrooms (or water closets as they were known) were first incorporated into the homes of high-income families, they were generally quite large. Tubs were often freestanding, with the Victorian claw-foot tub, made from solid cast iron with a porcelain interior being a popular model. Toilets were heavily embellished with relief-style or painted decorations and ornamentation often borrowed from the baroque. Embossed tiles or wooden wainscoting were employed, and the room was colorful, decorative and cheerful. Typical Victoriana, you could say.

During the 20th century, the bathroom gradually diminished in size, became more utilitarian and — in recent times — has favored straight, clean lines. Now, this is all beginning to change again with the introduction of a more freeform, open plan aesthetic; as a result, freestanding tubs are experiencing a resurgence in popularity.

In addition to the vintage tub, with its solid brass fittings and ball-in-claw feet, there is any number of modern permutations to choose from. Some take their design inspiration from Roman times: classical rounded forms that are both elegant and historical. Others are abso-lutely contemporary, often double ended in style. Whichever you opt for, give it precedence in your new, spacious bathroom. Mount the tub on a pedestal in the middle of the room so that it becomes the center of attention and arrange the other fixtures and fittings around it. Tables, bookshelves and even a comfy lounger are optional extras.

Our selection showcases some of the more modern styles of free-standing tubs, but, as you can see, all are placed in rooms of some substance. This extra size gives more freedom in the placement of amenities; add a floor-to-ceiling mirror and you end up with twice the space again.

Clockwise from left A modern artwork, huge mirror and flat-screen TV give this bathroom at Singapore's New Majestic hotel a multi-faceted look; cool tones and simple geometric shapes give this wet room a roomy but minimalistic feel; claw-foot tub in brass is illuminated by just the right amount of light from teak louvered shutters at Spa Botanica, Singapore; by keeping the hardware outside the tub, this modern design allows for comfortable bathing; this Mandala Spa bathroom in Boracay combines rusticity (thatch and rubble walls) with modernity (state-of-the art Jacuzzi tub).

THE TROPICAL POOL

No longer simple watering holes, today's tropical pools pay homage to imaginative aquatic designers and the beauty of the settings they find themselves in. A well-designed swimming pool sits in its environment like a hand in a glove: It looks like it has always been there.

Be it starkly geometric, free-form or infinity edge, the pool needs to be properly in proportion to the home and garden. Avoid overshadowing architecture with a huge pool; equally well, we don't want the needle in a haystack effect. Look at the contours of the topography, the possibilities for poolside plantings, and the relationship between the site of the pool and the site of the house.

In this chapter, we give you plenty of information and inspiration on pool types, shapes, colors and materials, as well as top tips on outdoor lighting and land-scaping. Our references always hark back to iconic pool designs in some of the tropical world's finest resorts and hotels — the Alila Ubud's jutting into the jungle number designed by Kerry Hill and Ed Tuttle's cascading waterfall effect at Amankila immediately spring to mind. We also like the way many landscapers and pool designers integrate swimming pools with reflecting pools and lily ponds; take a look at The Balé in Bali or some of landscape architect Martin Palleros's works.

And, even though sunbathing is less popular these days, there has to be space for poolside lounging both in the sun and shade. Don't be confused by the seemingly limitless choice for outdoor furniture though: be guided by how hard-wearing and weather-resistant the materials are, as well as what sort of look you want to achieve. Be it sleek and modernist or more traditional and softer-lined, there is a plethora of durable furniture around. Go for snythetic rattan weaves that resist both heat and intense ultraviolet light, webbed aluminum, sturdy cast-iron, and Sunbrella fabrics that don't fade, so you don't have to lug loungers and tables out of the garden during the night or when it rains.

Chinese geomancy or *feng shui* was an important consideration in the design of this pool and "floating" *lanai* (deck or verandah) at the home of Rikki Dee in the Philippines. Designed by Ed Ledesma of Locsin Partners, the travertine water-wall brings the harmonious notes of trickling water into the equation, while breezes flow through billowing drapes on the *lanai*. Sturdy modern furniture in the form of a high-backed Philippe Starck sofa and boxy poufs were chosen by the owner, a design aficionado.

Top Even though the lagoon with its crystal clear sea water is super appealing here, it is the accents that make the scene — the simple sun shades, the rugged deck and the elegant teak loungers.

Above A natural plunge pool built between boulders at aptly named Rock Villa affords splendid views out to Nanh Van Bay in Vietnam. Seemingly rough and ready furniture made from recycled wood fits the overall look.

INFINITE
POSSIBILITIES

There's nothing quite like the sea in the tropics: with more than a couple of different dozen shades of blue — from transparent to cerulean to turquoise, to slate grey streaked with white, to milky blue and cobalt — it is as expressive as the names of its numerous colors. In the same way that the Eskimos have over 30 names for 'snow', surely Asia has the same for 'sea' — and if it doesn't, it should.

Wherever you go — an atoll in the Maldives, a beach in Bali, a Thai idyll — you have a myriad different impressions of what is essentially the same thing: the sea. Combine this ever-changing pantone panorama with an infinity pool and an endless sky — and you have your design canvas to build on. You'll only need a few additional elements: a bit of bleached wood decking, a couple of slender palms, maybe a sleek lounger or two. White works well with blue, of course — think pristine fluffy towels, floaty drapes in soft Indian cotton, and the foam of crashing waves.

Of course, not many of us have a prime beachfront plot on a private island, but let's — for a moment — expand the range of possibilities and pretend that we do. Let's sketch the expansive curve of the pool edge, line it with the half-moon shape of the bay and make sure it is just the correct height to allow the pool edge to merge with the sea. Lift the cornea a touch, and allow it to rest on where horizon meets sky — and it's as though the blue stretches on forever.

Such spatial sensations are at the heart of infinity edge pool design. The primary aim is to create the idea of an open body of water that is seemingly endless. On a smaller, more realistic scale, such pools can work well in private homes without sea views — and can even be incorporated into a completely level garden. As they draw the eye toward and over the edge of the swimming pool, a well-placed piece of art, a dramatic sculpture or a specimen tree can take the place of the sea. The reflection of this primary focal point forms a secondary focal point on the surface of the water — and another illusion is created.

Left The stunning infinity edge pool at Villa Beige in Koh Samui is made from natural travertine stone with a special waterproof finish on top. Lined by modernist loungers from Dedon in Vietnam, it forms a poetic picture in blue. Dedon loungers are made from a highly durable synthetic fiber that is not affected by salt water, sunlight and high temperatures, so they are ideally suited to this tropical outpost. The covers are also made from a water-resistant fabric.

Below An infinity edge pool can also work well with a jungle or garden backdrop. This pool at the photogenic Tirta Ening Villa at Como Shambhala Estate in Bali seems to float above its garden setting, much as old Javanese homes did above their water gardens. The sleek wood-shingle roofed poolside pavilion adds a Japanese element.

FREE FORM **POOLS**

In the old days, swimming pools were about 20-foot by 40-foot and rectangular in shape.
They had a shallow end and a deep end with a diving board. They were functional and fun, but
that was about it.

Over the years, aquatic designers have taken the plunge and broken out of this standard box.
Eschewing the straightlaced rectangle or square for wavy, freeform models, often on multi levels,
they've taken pool design into a different sphere. Integration with the landscape and the outline
of the land, taking into account the shape and style of the home, evaluating the views or possible
views — all these considerations, as well as the actual shape of the pool, define this new approach.

The result has been nothing short of startling. We now see pools with islands, adjacent fire pits or
amoeba shapes; split-level infinity edged numbers; curvy contoured and sexy styles; weirs, water-
falls and water features . . . you name it, the pool has become multi-faceted.

Circular pool forms work best when they contrast with geometric architecture. If your home is
modern, stark and austere, it could benefit from a sinuous pool form. Give definition to the curves
by edging the pool in a stone color and texture that contrasts with the tiles; add some more
texture with softening tropical plantings; and — if there is room — plan it over different levels.
However, you'll need to keep a connection between home, garden and pool: this may be achieved
by continuity in paving and decking, and a structured approach to the choice of plants.

Our examples run the gamut from labyrinthine and long, to rounded and cascading. Jungle or
seaside settings with views to die for help, of course, but aren't essential. More important is an eye
for proportion and a commitment to individuality.

Above left Blending seamlessly with its site, this
pretty Jacuzzi pool at the Four Seasons Jimbaran
Bay in Bali is tranquil and cool. Imaginative
landscaping with flame-red russelia and
assorted mini trees including a sculptural
pandanus is by Madé Wijaya.

Above Aiming for harmony between natural site and architecture, GM Architects has expressively made this pool organically shaped to contrast with the sleek lines of the multi-roofed villa. A curvy path lines the water's edge, then changes direction at the narrowest point to lead visitors to the villa entrance. The interaction between the various shapes and volumes is an important part of the concept design.

Above right This design by Bill Bensley for the Anantara group merges a freeform infinity edge pool with a vast lagoon dotted with water lilies. The references hark back to Thai water garden culture, interpreted in a contemporary idiom.

Right Carefully selected materials characterise and delineate this Balinese watering hole — *palimanan* pool edge, pebblewash paving, white pebbles, timber decking and limestone on the perimeter wall.

CUBES OF COOL

The rectangular swimming pool — be it an eight-lane utility in a sports club or long and thin for lap enthusiasts at home — is the most common shape for a pool. However, ubiquitous does not have to preclude unique: Think of Kerry Hill's much-copied azure cube of cool in the Alila Ubud or the four-lane Olympic size pool in New York's art deco Downtown Athletic Club. Sited on the 12th-floor, it sits beneath a double-height ceiling and has been described as a "metropolitan *pièce-de-résistance*" by architect Rem Koolhaas.

That said, you're not likely to site your pool in a skyscraper or a pristine jungle setting. Far more likely (and prosaically), it will be in the garden on a flat piece of land near the house. But this doesn't mean that it has to be simple, or boring, or both.

Starkly geometric pools can look extraordinary if they are set at an angle from the house, if they jut out over a ridge (preferably with an infinity edge), or if they sink down into the ground so as to almost disappear within the landscape. Clever use of mosaic tiles, definition edging, attractive planting and lines of modernist loungers can lift even the simplest of designs. Size is another factor: oversized pools can up the wow factor purely in terms of scale.

A couple of things to note about rectangular pools: Expect to pay more for a rectangular pool than a curved-shape pool as most builders price a pool on the length of the perimeter. Also, note the importance of space around the pool: you'll need a deck or paved area — for access, safety and aesthetics. Most aquatic designers recommend the area surrounding the pool be at least equal to the size taken for the pool itself. And, if small children are involved, a safety fence is a must; some countries have strict laws on pools, gates and grills.

Left top A villa in Downtown Apartments in Bali on a small plot looks spacious and attractive through clever space planning. The slate and wood water feature at the end elongates the pool, while the deck on left and sculptural planting on right doesn't take up too much square footage. There is even room for an entertainment area.

Above Retro pool tiles contrast with a modernist fountain designed by architect Miguel Pastor at the home of Ben Chan in the Philippines. Similarly the arty big lips sofa in crimson on the deck contrasts with a moss-encrusted urn filled with water plants.

Left Architecture, plantings and pool are sensitively arranged by Sim Boon Yang of eco-id design consultancy on what is essentially a small plot in Singapore. On right, the "wall" of the living room opens up completely to allow access to the pool, while a stand of bamboo offers privacy opposite. At the far end of the pool, there's another large opening into the house and a small deck for outdoor dining.

Opposite bottom A balance of horizontal and vertical lines characterises this sleek pool and garden designed by Martin Palleros of Tierra Design for a condo in Singapore. The pool is set at an angle to the perimeter grey stone wall punctuated with green plants, while the long slim deck follows faithfully the pool's edge.

Left Atmospheric night lighting at Shreyas, near Bangalore in India, is achieved here through three sources — pretty paper candle lanterns lining the pool edge, underwater illumination and long thin outdoor lights attached to the adjacent building wall. The combination of electric and candle lighting makes for moving shadows and beautiful reflections. **Right** Downlighting on the home, spots below the frangipani tree and further outdoor lights hanging in the tree, as well as a backlit screen at the far end of the pool, provide the nighttime illumination around this courtyard pool in Bangkok. The attractive flower arrangement submersed in a large acrylic vase on left is lit by flickering floating candles.

NIGHT LIGHTS

Many people overlook lighting, both inside and outside the home, when they're designing a space. It is often the last consideration, when really it should be one of the first. After all, clever lighting creates atmosphere, casts emphasis on particular elements or areas, and provides drama, especially outdoors.

If you have a pool, a deck and a garden, you'll need different types of lights for each of these three areas. The trick is to avoid glare — at all costs. And remember, there will be some light overspill coming from the rooms inside that will be visible outside, so take this into consideration in the planning stages. You want soft, subdued illumination, not bright burn-the-eyeballs light.

Two factors are paramount: safety and aesthetics. The former is achieved with step lights and path lights, as well as lights in such spots as barbecue grills; the latter can utilize a wide variety of lights — pendant and spot lights, outdoor wall lights, and lights in and around your pool.

One of the most colorful and safest methods of lighting up a swimming pool is with fiber optic pool lights that have no electricity running through them. Water and electricity are a deadly combination, so fiber optics ensure all the power components are contained in an area isolated from the pool. Other alternatives include underwater halogen lights — they have the advantage of running costs at about a third of conventional lights — and LED lights which come in a variety of colors.

Solar lights are also easy-to-use and safe in the garden. They operate from renewable energy and are wireless, so they may be manipulated and moved around the garden at will. Newer models are proving longer lasting and brighter (but more expensive) than some of the previous types on the market, so they're something to consider.

As for styles — make sure the shapes, materials and sizes are in keeping with your general home theme. Modern and sleek go with clutter-free environments, while traditional models are more suitable for cottage-style homes with "messier" gardens.

Far left Illumination around this small plunge pool at Ayana Villa comes from spots in the adjacent ceiling and light from the deck. The pool itself has been left au naturel.

Left If you haven't budgeted for pool lights, there are a number of floating lights on the market that produce a variety of different atmospheres and colors; some are solar powered — they recharge whilst floating about the pool during the day, then put on a spectacular light-and-color show at night.

THE PAVILION BY THE POOL

Pavilions have a long history in Asia. With their roots in sacred buildings (the Javanese *pendopo* is a good example), utilitarian structures (the Thai *sala* as the equivalent of the bus shelter aside the *klong* or canal) and social spaces (the Balinese *balé* as meeting place), they come in all shapes and sizes. And because of their architectural suitability to the tropics, they have been adopted, adapted and re-invented in many a tropical home.

Pavilions can be used as semi open-air dining rooms in a verdant garden or as viewing platforms with floor cushions or loungers. Suitable for siestas, they allow breezes to enter, but keep the equatorial sun and rain at bay. After all, every rice field in Bali has a *balé* offering farmers respite in relative comfort between back-breaking work in the fields. In modern villas and homes, however, it is poolside that the pavilion really comes into its own.

Here, it acts as a natural adjunct to cooling waters. Far more effective than even the largest of large umbrellas, it allows those of us who eschew the sun for shade to relax without having to head indoors. Furnished simply with bamboo loungers or comfy floor-level cushions, the poolside pavilion may also house pool essentials — cool drinks from a small fridge, towels, swimming gear and pool cleaning equipment. As with all great design, the Asian pavilion combines functionality with form — it is both practical and beautiful.

For larger structures, we recommend eight posts or even 12 posts and a tiled or wood-shingled roof; this incurs less maintenance over the years and mitigates problems with tropical bugs. Smaller pavilions can look quaint and homey with thatched roofs, carved posts and reed matting floors on a raised platform. Steps are optional — and the degree of sophistication depends on your garden and pool's overall style statement. Keep it rustic and simple if you are going for a thrown-together look (the pool should also be *au naturel*, possibly amoeba shaped with artfully placed boulders and plantings); and if you want sleek, modern lines, go for tiles, geometric shapes, canvas awnings, and the latest in pared-down, clean-lined outdoor furniture.

Above left Poolside at Ayana Villa offers several lounging options, beneath the *alang-alang* roofs of two typical Balinese *balés* or on elegant curvy teak loungers under the sun.

Above right A typical Balinese *balé* at Spa Village Resort Tembok, Bali offers views over both ocean and pool; the addition of soft drapes gives privacy for an afternoon siesta.

Far left More covered daybed than pavilion, this poolside lounger is a picture in carved teakwood and soft natural cotton.

Middle left A multi-tiered, elaborate pavilion at Chiang Mai's Dhara Dhevi takes its inspiration from Burmese temple forms.

Left Boxy modernist *balé* at The Balé seems to float at the pool's end. The mix of smooth limestone and rubble walls, as well as wooden decking and choice landscaping gives this swimming pool a tranquil air.

THE TROPICAL POOL

Right A collaboration between landscaper Frank Borja and architect Jorge Yulo served to create the tranquil feeling around this pool in Manila. House cladding in chipped granite, green-grey pool tiles and stands of slender oriental bamboo are perfect pool mates.
Far right Mosaics both within the pool and without, a stand of spiny palms, and original colorful windows form an intriguing scenario at this rooftop pool at the New Majestic in Singapore. Cute portholes (unseen) give views to diners in the restaurant below.

Far left A guest house designed by landscape artist Ponce Veridiano in the Laguna area of the Philippines utilizes plants that thrive in the area's slightly high elevation: giant tree ferns, bamboos and the like.
Left White bougainvillea and white frangipani work with *paras Jogja* stone and acqua blue tiles in this stunning villa at The Balé. The landscaping was by Karl Princic who wanted the villa to appear as if it were carved out of the hillside.

POOLSIDE **PLANTINGS**

Landscape designers in the tropics tend to fall into one of two categories: the modernist less-is-more type and the luxuriant, layered and artfully natural genre. The former type leans towards a Zen-inspired, rigorous approach, whilst the latter joyfully celebrates the abundance of tropical plants, delighting in their plethora of color, texture, variety and forms.

Personal inclination plays a large role in which "camp" you fall into, but, when considering the choice of plants and styles for poolside landscaping, your solution will largely be dictated by the architecture of your home and the shape, size and extent of the pool. A rectilinear, modern home often benefits from a curvy pool with a jungle-scape style of landscape; a more geometric pool may work better with neatly regimented rows of sculptural plants.

Other factors to take into account are the choice of hardscapes around the pool, the size of the garden, what other water features — if any — are involved, and how the architecture and landscaping can be integrated and incorporated together. Many projects, unfortunately, leave the landscaping budget to the end; then, when the money has run out, the garden is cobbled together. Not a good plan!

Consulting an experienced landscape designer is obviously a good starting point, but studying different plants, combinations of plants, the textures of stone, wood, plants and so on, as well as colors of blooms, can help you formulate your preferences. We showcase a few different styles here: minimalist, mosaic and sculptural at the New Majestic hotel in Singapore; hardscape-driven at The Balé in Bali; clean-lined and cute in a Filipino garden; and luxuriant and textured, yet still tidy and tamed, in a private garden also in the Philippines.

For full-on, artful naturalism, refer specifically to the gardens, water courts and poolscapes of landscape designer Madé Wijaya. If anyone can create a layered look, a surprise around every corner, a deceptively engineered yet constantly-changing garden — it is this master of tropical gardening.

POOLSIDE FURNITURE

Everybody's dream vacation on a tropical island includes sun-drenched vistas of pool, ocean and horizon. Also included are idyllic scenes of lounging poolside, with a book, a cold scented towel and not a worry in the world.

For such a scenario, a good lounger is a must. Plastic struts that stick to skin, hard wooden numbers that dig you in the backbone, slimy covers that slip and slide … it's easy to describe the ones that we don't like. But the perfect lounger, shaped to support the contours of the back, not too hard, not too soft — does such a thing exist?

Well, yes and no. Some such as the timeless PK24 lounger designed in the middle of the last century by Poul Kjaerholm (a disciple of Hans Wegner) and still manufactured by Danish brand Fritz Hansen meets the comfort and sustainability criteria, but falls short on outdoor practicality. So does the iconic Le Corbusier LC4: These are better suited to verandahs or living rooms than pool decks.

For an outdoor lounger, weather resistance, portability and timeless design are key. Recent technological advances have resulted in the manufacture of a number of different styles of lightweight loungers — look for resin or polyurethane wicker weave models on a vinyl frame; sturdy resin loungers that have back adjustability and two back wheels for ease of maneuver; and aluminum loungers with a porotex mesh back and seat. Natural woods, such as sustainable bamboo and rattan also work, as long as the materials have a waterproof coating. All these are elegant and aesthetic, and wear very well.

They also work well without cushions which is a boon, because however hard-wearing your fabric is, cushions tend to fade and go moldy in the tropics. If you do opt for outdoor cushions, cover them in Sunbrella fabrics: Originally designed for up-market yachts, they are virtually weatherproof and also help to filter out the sun's harmful rays. How cool is that?

Opposite top and bottom Two styles of pool furniture by Filipino designer Antonio "Budji" Layug — an adapted hammock and a lounger. Layug is famous for furniture pieces that utilize native materials — hardwood and hemp, bamboo, rattan, *abaca* and more — that are executed in modern, sleek styles. Craftsmanship is always a priority as is functionality. "What excites me is the discovery of a material that can be interpreted into a new design and shape, and bring new meaning to its use today," he says.
Above The fabric on both the bed and lounger here is water- and sun-resistant. Beige is a sensible shade for the tropics, as it stays cool and won't lose its color.
Right Rustic-style bamboo loungers and side tables on the terrace of Ilocos sandstone at the home of Ponce Veridiano in Laguna, the Philippines. Although bamboo is an eco-friendly and reasonably hard-wearing choice, such loungers won't last long if left outside to absorb the vagaries of the tropical climate. It is recommended they are stored under cover when not in use.

THE TROPICAL GARDEN

Tropical gardens can be as simple or as complicated as you want them to be. There's no one size fits all in this department. As we're not experts in plants and plantings, we won't delve into the myriad choices you have in that department. What we will do, however, is give you some ideas for materials, features and vantage points from where you can sit to enjoy the garden view.

Courtyards, patios and verandahs are key in the design of a tropical house and garden. Often these comprise part of the home via a series of interconnecting spaces where you can enjoy both indoors and outdoors. If they are stand-alone features, there will still be some sort of umbilical pull to the house. It may take the form of a cloistered walkway or a pathway or may simply be a focus where the eye falls when looking out.

Materials are paramount here: You need to choose hard-wearing stone or wood that doesn't become slippy during rain or discolor too much with intense heat. Resin covered cement, scored before it sets, is a modern option that always looks cool underfoot. If you are going for tiles or paving, don't let the pattern get too busy, as it will prove too disconcerting to the eye. Similarly, if opting for wooden decking, get it waterproofed and treated first. And remember to soften these areas with plenty of plants — shade-giving shrubs, flowering ornamentals in planter boxes or beds, cool water features and hard-wearing outdoor furniture.

Water features — reflecting pools, lily ponds, water walls, fountains — go hand in hand with tropical gardens. Not only are they aesthetic, they are practical too; as air blows over their surfaces, it cools and brings welcome breeze to stuffy corners. In addition, the sound of trickling or flowing water is comforting and relaxing. Most tropical landscapers wouldn't consider designing a garden without some kind of water garden. Be it a streamlined, plant-less hardscape, or a softer freeform shape with water vegetation, it is a welcome addition to a tropical scene.

As is a comfy lounger, planter's chair, bench or hammock. After all, we always need somewhere to slumber and sip iced tea whilst admiring the view, don't we?

The entrance to the Balinese home of two ceramic artists is a picture of symmetry. The pathway is made from sand-cast ceramic tiles in relief set in a bed of grey pebbles, while sculptural agaves and manicured lawn add the necessary green.

WATER FEATURES **AND PONDS**

A fusion of exotic tropical ornamentals with European concepts of landscape design constitutes what today we term a "tropical garden". Add to that the speed with which plants grow in the tropics, constant heat, plentiful rainfall and rich soil — and you have the reasons why so many people harbor hopes of transforming their back yard into a paradisiacal space. It's not too difficult if you put your mind to it. One of the integral elements of such a dream Garden of Eden is a water feature — or two.

Today, many of the region's top names in landscape design tend to favor water features that are clean-lined and fuss-free, often eschewing plants entirely and replacing them with a floating pavilion, a statue or an oversized lamp (see below). They specifically take into account what is reflected within the water, rather than what is around it, often taking into account Eastern concepts of *feng shui*. Others, however, cannot resist the softening, organic effect of rampant tropical planting; while the water feature itself may indeed be formal or geometric, it is surrounded by a profusion of foliage (see far right). Another favorite these days is the sculptural water wall: Made from rough-hewn granite, textured travertine, stacked tiles or some different stone, they are built so as to allow water to ripple over their surface for pleasing visual and aural effect.

Fountains, spouts, water bubblers, cascades and rills are other popular choices. Featuring in Persian, Roman, Arab and Greek gardens, they were embraced by the Anglo-Saxons whose expansive country estates were never without an ornate fountain or two. Today's Asian gardens may not have the scale of such ancient water gardens, but they'll use statuary and urns, pools and ponds, for the same effect — to act as a balm to the mind and soul. The sound of water immediately creates a feeling of tranquility, as the Japanese and Chinese well knew: They used water, stone, plants and architecture (opposing *yin* and *yang* forces) to create an all-encompassing feeling of tranquility. Try some of our ideas to do just that.

Far left Water within water: Designed by Yasuhiro Koichi of Spin Design but realized by glass artist Seiki Torige, a beautifully rotund glass lantern/fountain ball is placed within a limestone square that is itself placed over a shallow pond made from black granite with a pointed hammered finish. The effect is mesmerising especially at night when the acqua balls glow and seem to "float" on the pond.

Middle left A modern take on Chinese *feng shui* at the entrance to a home in Singapore designed by Sim Boon Yang of eco-id design consultancy. Guarded by two 11th century Cambodian lions, visitors literally have to step over water to enter.

Left Placing a pond adjacent the verandah ensures the entrance of cooling breezes. A shallow urn at center adds the gentle sound of trickling water too.

Above left The owner of this transplanted 150-year-old Toba Batak house admits freely that she borrowed the idea for her forecourt with circular wooden staircase surrounding a lily pond from Don Jaime Zobel's rustic Mindoro home high above Puerta Galera. The coal-filled giant shell sculpture at center blazes from dusk until dawn, lighting the way for visitors.

Above right Order combines with chaos for a type of "chaotic order" here: Geometric connecting pools, spouts, urns and ponds mix with a profusion of low-lying bird's nest ferns, spathiphyllum and a bed of pebbles for an organic and balanced composition. Interestingly this is an interior garden which was created by Sitthiporn Dhonavanik, one of Thailand's top landscape designers.

Left A small area between this urban home's external wall and living room is filled with the addition of a cooling rectangular pool with freeform tree.

Below The entrance to Ku De Ta, a restaurant in Bali, was designed and realized by stone mason Richard North-Lewis. Taking inspiration from the modern library in Alexandria and New York subway grafitti, the concept is nevertheless rooted in Chinese *feng shui* precepts. The concrete fountain is set in a bed of pebbles from Flores.

Left Eschewing such outdated concepts as tradition and architectural regionalism for what he calls "development", Dutch-Thai architect Hans Brouwer builds for the future. This rigorous water feature in a villa he designed in Singapore is a study in light, geometry and texture.

Below The entrance to the spa at the Farm at San Benito features a severe grey pebblewash forecourt with black granite fountain surrounded by large grey stones. Grey wood shingle roofs echo the general tone of measured, balanced tranquility.

GARDEN **WALKWAYS**

Concrete — polished, set in relief, brushed or scored — is increasingly proving popular for both tropical garden hardscapes and flooring within the home. Its cool feel beneath the feet, especially when coated with resin, is a balm on a hot day. However, there are plenty of other options to consider for a garden walkway: treated wood, natural stone, pebblewash tiles, granite and andesite, limestone, terracotta and bricks.

The three Ps are important with paving stones: practicality, pattern and proportion. First of all the pavers must be non-slip, rot-resistant, have good drainage and be placed close enough together so that you don't have to jump from one stone to the next. This last point may seem obvious, but how often have you had to change your stride on a garden path or stop mid flight, as it were, on a flight of roughly-hewn garden stairs? Secondly, when devising the pattern — the way the slabs interact or are arranged — don't become over ambitious and arty. You'll end up with a walkway that is too busy and confusing, not easy on the eye or under foot. Finally, think about how your garden path is going to relate to the environment in which it sits. What is its primary aim? Where is it leading? What is around it? Try to harmonize it with the architecture, trees, plantings and any water features you are planning for.

A trend that is proving increasingly popular is the placement of paving slabs, be they natural rocks, tiles or paving stones, on a variety of backgrounds. We give illustrations of pavers in a bed of pebbles, crossing over water, in a lawn and over other hardscapes. See what you think of them.

Above left The owner of this home in Thailand used white pavers set at angles on an emerald green lawn to mark a route from house to relaxation daybed. The contrast of both colors and textures is eye-catching.

Above middle GM Architects designed home in Bali uses natural elements, such as water in the form of lily pond, roughly hewn stepping stones and wood shingle tiles on roof as a counterpoint to severely geometric architecture. This path forms a dramatic entranceway.

Above right The living room and pool are connected by a lily pond traversed by sturdy wooden planks at this Singapore home.

Right A connecting path at the Aramsa Spa in Singapore is composed of different shaped stone pavers set in grey pebbles. Abundant foliage around makes for a natural scene.

Far right Moss-encrusted mini walls line a gently descending pebbledash pathway leading to the garden at the Farm at San Benito.

Top A Laguna verandah sports a newly restored bench with attached curvy table and planter's chair set on a polished concrete floor. The traditional fabric cushions have been treated with a coating to help elongate their life.
Above Bangkok-based furniture designer Rangsan Narathasajan is one of a new breed of creative cognoscenti that uses new materials but produces designs that are rooted in the traditions of his native Thailand. Manually woven high grade UPVC fiber forms the base for these two sofas that are shaped in the form of a *kwien*, a cart used by Thai farmers. Similarly, the two small tables are inspired by the *keang*, a traditional Thai chopping board. Weather resistant covers are in Sunbrella fabrics and the deck is made from sustainable *teng* wood. At Shasa Samui boutique hotel in Koh Samui, Thailand.

SITTING PRETTY

Verandahs, decks, patios, gardens and gazebos have been experiencing a facelift in recent years with the advent of a plethora of new outdoor furniture designs. Not only are the shapes and styles sexier, the actual fabrics and forms have undergone a radical makeover.

Whilst teak and wrought iron have traditionally monopolized the outdoor furniture market, we are seeing more pieces made from sustainable timbers with a protective finish and rust-proofed and/or powder-coated wrought aluminum. Mesh-and-metal is also seeing a resurgence as it allows for air circulation — even with a towel on top, a lounger with a mesh body is able to "breathe".

Somehow, sitting on a tropical verandah taking in exuberant garden views is more alluring when done from a chair that hasn't decimated a 1,000-year-old forest! The new wave of furniture designers tends to employ sensitive production practices using tropical hardwoods only when salvaged and recycled; alternatively, they're replacing them with sustainable timbers such as bamboo. Woven materials — cane, wicker, rattan and water hyacinth — are upgraded by being combined with something more water- and weather-resistant. And for a fresh new look, traditional materials may be teamed with modern accessories or combined with other materials such as glass, aluminum, ceramic and the like. They're also being paired with new, more weather-resistant covers. Marine grade vinyls and acrylic fabrics that don't rot or fade are replacing traditional ikat, batik and cotton. Such fabric also dries quickly, so it's a great boon in equatorial monsoon conditions.

Of course, there are plenty of antiques around too. These are constantly recycled — strengthened and sanded, re-stained and restored in the many ateliers that dot the tropical world. In an area where the jungle gives up its bounty, sometimes willingly sometimes not, it would be criminal not to utilize what's on offer, wouldn't it?

Above The home of Tina Maristela-Ocampo and Ricco Ocampo in Manila is a showcase of innovative design. Their *lanai* combines hard and soft textures, the man-made with the organic, via strictly modernist mid-century Lucite sofas contrasting with fossilized Indonesian tree trunk tables sporting shell decoration and capiz shell covered hanging lamps from Pampanga province.
Below A timeless northern Thai scene on the Chiang Mai balcony of Ajahn Chulathat Kittibutr. The beautiful contours of a traditional teak lounger and

stool match the balcony's perforated wooden railings, a common feature in Shan and Lanna houses. Recycled teak taken from abandoned houses and barns is used throughout.
Below A formal Thai garden with clipped topiary trees and regimented rows of shrubs in contrasting colors is fronted by a neat lawn on which is placed a traditional teak bench. The splendid blue-grey palm behind is a *Bismarckia nobilis*, native to the island of Madagascar.

Right Modern outdoor furniture by Dedon uses a synthetic weave and tough grey cushions for weather-resistance on a partially covered *lanai* in Manila. The grey tones of upholstery and floor are given a lift by vibrant plantings of alocasia, still in their infancy. Decor and garden designed by Ramon Antonio.

Bottom left European-style bench with wooden slats on a cast-iron base with elegant legs sits in a garden court surrounded with stands of bamboo. The prettily patterned central feature was executed using a pebbledash technique (the art of placing stones into a bed of mortar over a concrete base).

Bottom right Lush dining corner at the Farm at San Benito features a somewhat treacherous floor covered with a carpet of moss. Rustic, practical furniture sits beneath a 200-year-old mango tree that has become draped over time with a type of hanging moss.

Above A cosy corner at the home of Laura and Ronnie Rodrigo in Manila features a custom-crafted, low lounger that comfortably sits three or four beneath an ancient *balete* tree. A tribal mortar and pestle with carved figure sits behind a modern sculpture.

Right The garden of Ponce Veridiano, a well-known landscape designer in the Philippines, is engulfed with bamboos, giant ferns, bromeliads and various flowering ornamentals that thrive in the elevated conditions in Nagcarlan, Laguna. Here, along a meandering path, set with Ilocos sandstone pavers, we find a resting point in the form of Chinese glazed ceramic stools around an antique sugar grinder that doubles up as a table.

Left In recent years, the island of Cebu in the Philippines has been dubbed the "Milan of Asia" because of its expanding and increasingly innovative furniture design and manufacturing businesses. Embracing new technologies, yet utilizing ethnic materials and craftsmanship, the pieces are lauded for their East meets West styles, as evidenced by this romantic canopied sofa and matching side table by Dedon.
Below Award-winning furniture designer Clayton Tugonon of Cebu is the mastermind behind this low-level natural coco chaise with swirling laminated pattern which he calls the "Low Sexy Chair". It is sold through the DeeFusion brand.

NEW DIRECTIONS IN
TROPICAL FURNITURE

In Asia, many tried-and-tested outdoor furniture designs continue to retain their popularity, despite the advent of new forms and materials. After all, who can claim to be immune to the allure of the old-fashioned tropical verandah? Planters' chairs, rattan loungers, cane-and-wood combos, as well as the ubiquitous woven hammock — all have a historic and enduring appeal.

Nevertheless, times change and designers cannot help but push boundaries and experiment with new forms and materials. The biggest development in recent years has been the emergence of a number of neo-weaves made from synthetic materials such as melamine, PVC fibers and polycarbonate. Resistant to rain, UV damage, wind and dust, they are hard-wearing and sustainable — factors that resonate with buyers today. Of particular note is so-called synthetic wicker: specifically designed to look like wicker yet wear like iron, it is woven with stainless-steel wires coated with resin and polyester. Mounted on aluminum frames, synthetic wicker outdoor furniture pieces look like the real thing.

Even though there are technical constraints inherent in such materials, we're seeing some beautiful contemporary designs with clean lines and an intelligent fusion of materials. There are both linear and rounded shapes, in dark, light and color dye-ed shades. Cushions and coverings are increasingly in Sunbrella fabrics (Sunbrella is a company that developed a fabric that that doesn't fade with chlorine and sun exposure). When a dark sofa, lounger or chair is teamed with light or neon colored Sunbrella textiles, the effect can be very appealing. Take a look at the collections — all Asia-made — we showcase here.

Above A home in Koh Samui, built on a hillside up high, has wonderful views out to sea. The rounded contours of modern neo-weave furniture echoes the shape of the boulders that scatter the topography of the site (unseen here but viewable on pages 24 and 49).
Below Another Cebu native, a dark bulbous pod of a sofa with matching side table, is both hard-wearing and aesthetically pleasing.

Below "A total design approach from exterior to interior is essential in creating a style that will endure the passage of time," says designer Antonio "Budji" Layug. Here, he places his design classic, the Cluster Bamboo table, on an outdoor terrace with light and airy tropical Carlotta Host chairs.

GARDEN SCULPTURES AND ACCENTS

In the same way that temple ornamentation is utilized within the home as interior decor, we often see the use of temple statues in the garden as a form of outdoor decoration. Be it the sinuous form of Dewi Saraswati, the Balinese goddess of the arts, a Buddha statue or head, a Thai or Khmer *deva* or deity seems irrelevant. As long as the statue is suitably moss-encrusted or has achieved a beautiful patina with age, its provenance is often ignored.

Garden art, of course, is nothing new. Populating courts with such statues, as well as bas reliefs of epic scenes inspired by those as seen on Khmer temples, is not a particularly Asian tradition. Formal English gardens were full of life-sized statues — figurines of Greek and Roman gods and godesses, cherubs, cupids, mythical beasts and the like — and they also favored more prosaic items such as bird baths, sundials and urns. These are similarly popular in the tropics: you'll find many a courtyard garden filled to the brim with old glazed Chinese water carriers or giant terracotta indigo-dipping vats from Indonesia.

Garden accents often double up as fountains, lights, planters and receptacles for floral blooms (see right). There's many a Balinese and Javanese atelier churning out literally hundreds of terracotta and stone garden ornaments and urns daily. So, to avoid the obvious, choose carefully. Then place them carefully. They can be used as focal points, to divide up areas in a garden, to delineate spaces, or as flanking forms at an entranceway. Sometimes, it works to have groups of accents, rather than solitary items. We give you a few examples here.

Above One of two bronze mermaids that form a fountain in one of the most famous tropical gardens in the world — the Allerton Gardens in Hawaii. A masterpiece of tropical romanticism, the gardens were established in 1938 by industrialist Robert Allerton and his adopted son combining the basic tenets of the Renaissance garden with tropical plants and trees.
Right and opposite far right The garden of Edric Ong in Kuching is peopled with a number of wooden guardian figures from Sarawak and Kalimantan.

Middle left A Balinese deity statue is decorated with bright red hibiscus blooms.
Left The turtle is a symbol of longevity and steadfastness in north Asia (China, Vietnam, Korea, Japan), so is often found in temple courts. This statue welcomes guests to the home of landscaper Ponce Veridiano.
Above Decorative containers such as these make for attractive ornaments in a court or niche of a courtyard.

ACKNOWLEDGMENTS

The author and photographer would like to thank a great many people for their help during the production of this book. We apologize in advance if we have missed anybody out; the list is seemingly endless! Wherever possible, especially for suppliers, design companies and the like, we have given contact details.

Homes
Philippines—Ponce Veridiano; Anton R Mendoza; Charles and Ginnette Dumancas; Michael Pena; Laura and Ronnie Rodrigo; Tina Maristela-Ocampo and Ricco Ocampo; Ben Chan; Rikki Dee; Ana Rocha
Thailand—Vichien Chansevikul and Michael Palmer; Rika Dila; Robert Powell and Lieve Aerts-Powell; Karl Morsbach; Mark Talley; Ajahn Chulathat Kittibutr; Cindi Novkov
Bali—Frank Morgan; Carlo Pessina; Edith Jesuttis; Philip Lakeman and Graham Oldroyd; Anneke van Waesberghe
Vietnam—Catherine Denoual and Doan Dai Tu; Loan de Leo Foster; Quasar Khanh
Sarawak—Edric Ong
Singapore—Karina Zahibi and Robert Rigg; Cindy and Philip Jeyaretnam
Myanmar—Claudia and Patrick Robert

Hotels, Restaurants, Bars and Spas
Thailand—Oriental hotel (wwwmandarin oriental.com/bangkok); Mandarin Oriental Dhara Dhevi (www.mandarinoriental.com/chiangmai); Marriott Resort and Spa (www.marriott.com); Rachamankha Hotel (www.rachamankha.com); Anantara, Hua Hin and Golden Triangle (www. anantara.com); Amanpuri (www.amanresorts.com); Villa Beige (www.villabeige.com); Shasa Samui hotel (www.shasahotels.com)
Singapore—New Majestic hotel (www.new majestichotel.com); Naumi hotel (www.naumi hotel.com); Aramsa — the Garden Spa (www. aramsaspas.com); Spa Botanica, Sentosa Resort & Spa (www.spabotanica.com); Jim Thompson restaurant (www.jimthompson.com/restaurants_ bars/singapore)
Bali—Ku De Ta (www.kudeta.net); Four Seasons Resort Bali at Jimbaran Bay (www.fourseasons.com/ jimbaranbay); The Balé (www.thebale.com); Spa Village Resort Tembok, Bali (www.spavillage.com/ tembokbali); Como Shambhala Estate at Begawan Giri (www.cse.como.bz); Downtown Villas (www. downtownbali.com)
Maldives—Coco Palm Bodu Hithi (www.cocopalm. com)
India—Ananda (www.anandaspa.com); Shreyas Retreat (www.shreyasretreat.com); Park Hotel, New Delhi (www.theparkhotels.com)
Sri Lanka—Club Villa (www.club-villa.com); Sindbad Garden Hotel, Kalutara; Gallery Café, Colombo (www.paradiseroadsl.com/cafe)
Vietnam—Six Senses Hideaway Ninh Van Bay, (www.sixsenses.com))
The Philippines—Spider House, Boracay; Mandala Resort & Spa (www.mandalaspa.com); Manila Hotel (www.manila-hotel.com.ph); the Farm at San Benito (www.thefarm.com.ph)
China—Brilliant Resort, Kunming (www.slh.com/ peoples_republic_of_china/yunnan_province/ yunbri.html)

Museums and Gardens
Baba House Museum (www.nus.edu.sg/museum/ baba); Allerton Gardens (www.ntbg.org); Aguinaldo Shrine, Cavite; Jim Thompson House & Museum (www.jimthompsonhouse.com); The Braganza house, Chandor, Goa

Retailers/Designers
DeeFusion (www.deefusion.com); Dedon (www. dedon.de); Sifas (www.sifasusa.com); B&B Italia (www.bebitalia.it); Cappellini (www.cappellini.it); Minotti (www.minotti.it); Natuzzi (www.natuzzi. com); X•TRA Living (www.xtra.com.sg); Padua International (www.padua-intl.com); Mae Rim Ceramics (www.maerimceramic.com); Studio Naenna (www.studio-naenna.com); Gong Dee gallery (www.gongdeegallery.com); Mengrai Kilns (www.mengraikilns.com); Earth & Fire (www.aka- aka.com/earth_fire.html); AKA Chiang Mai (www. aka-aka.com/aka.html); Cocoon Design Co Ltd +66- 2 656-1007; Leather Paragon (www.leatherparagon. com); Villeroy & Boch (www.villeroy-boch.com); Jenggala Keramik (www.jenggala-bali. jenggala-bali. com); Space (www.spacefurniture.com.au); Fortuny (www.fortuny.com); Marimekko (www.marimekko. fi/eng); Jim Thompson — the Thai Silk Company (www.jimthompson.com); Celestina Maynila-New York (www.celestinamaynilanewyork.com); Pattaya Furniture Collection (www.pattayafur.com); Gaya Design (www.gayavietnam.com); Song Design (www.asiasongdesign.com); Celadon Green (+84-8 9144697)

Designers, Architects and Artists
Karina Zabihi of kzdesigns (www.kzdesigns.com); Sim Boon Yang and Calvin Sim of eco-id design consultancy (www.ecoid.com); Kevin Tan of aKTa-rchitects (www.akta.com.sg); Cheong Yew Kuan of Area Design (area@indo.net.id); Cindi Novkov; Bedmar & Shi (www.bedmar-and-shi.com); Jim Thompson Design Company (www.jimthompson. com); Joy Dominguez; Ponce Veridiano; Antonio 'Budji' Layug (www.budji.com); Clayton Tugonon; Gianni Franconi of G M Architects (giannfr@tin. it); Hans Breuer; Sitthiporn Dhonavanik; Ramon Antonio; Yasuhiro Koichi of Spin Design Studio (www.ds-spin.com); Seiki Torige at Galeri Esok Lusa (gundul@eksadata.com); Frank Borja; Jorge Yulo (www.jorgeyulo.com); Karl Princic at Karl Princic Design (kpd@dps.centrin.net.id); Martin Palleros of Tierra Design (www.tierradesign.com); Miguel Pastor; Bill Bensley of Bensley Design Studio (www. bensley.com); Ed Ledesma of Locsin Partners; Valentina Audrito (www.pianeta-sudest.com); Sakul Intakul (www.sakulintakul.com); Subodh Kerkar (www.subodhkerkar.co); Ana Rocha; Anneke van Waesberghe of Esprite Nomade (www. espritenomade.com); Made Wijaya of PT Wijaya Tribwana International (www.ptwijaya.com); Udom Udomsrianan; Rangsan Narathasajan; Le Cuong; Laki Senanayake (www.lakiarts.com); Udayshanth Fernando (www.paradiseroadsl.com); Barefoot (www.barefoot.lk); Linda Garland (www. panchoran-retreat.com); Borek Sipek (www.sipek.com); Joy Dominquez, Kathleen Henares; Anton R Mendoza (www.antonmendoza.com); Palmer & Turner; Leo Design